THE HISTORY OF
VIDEO
GAMES

SCHOLASTIC INC.

The Need for Speed 2

Tony Hawk's
Pro Skater

Dedicated to my kids, Joey and Janey,
and to video game-loving kids everywhere.

Special thanks to: Charlie Scibetta, Hana Bae, Stephenie Ly, Marc Boese,
Dan Pantumsinchai, Noriko Matsunaga, Brent Coyle, Tiffany O'Brien, Scott Jobe,
Barry MacDonald, and Grace Liu.

ISBN 978-0-545-88858-5

10 9 8 7 6 5 4 3 2 1   16 17 18 19 20

Printed in the U.S.A.   40

First edition, February 2016

Created & designed by Mojo-Media.com: Writer & Editor, Joe Funk; Writer, Trevor Talley;
Art Director, Daniel Tideman; Production Designer, Jason Shroyer

The Witche

CONTENTS

The First Games

It's easy to understand why people like video games: They're full of action and imagination—and they're fun to play! But video games are relatively new to the gaming world. People have played other games, such as cards, dice, board games, and sports, for thousands of years. In fact, some games are so old that we don't even know when they were invented.

Mongolian wrestling is a traditional sport that still takes place today.

GAME SYSTEM:

SPORTS

EARLIEST KNOWN EXAMPLE:
7000 BCE

WHERE WAS IT FOUND?
A cave in the Bayankhongor Province of Mongolia

WHAT WAS IT LIKE?
An ancient cave painting shows the earliest depiction of a sporting game—a wrestling match between two men with people looking on.

GAME SYSTEM:

DICE

EARLIEST KNOWN EXAMPLE:
3000 BCE

WHERE WAS IT FOUND?
The ruins of Başur Höyük, an ancient burial site located near the modern-day city of Siirt, in southeast Turkey

WHAT WAS IT LIKE?
Forty-nine stones carved in different shapes—some of which resemble modern dice—were found at the burial site. The find represents the earliest confirmed gaming items in the world.

GAME SYSTEM:

BOARD GAMES

EARLIEST KNOWN EXAMPLE:
2500 BCE

WHERE WAS IT FOUND?
Burial sites dating back to about 2500 BCE in what is now modern-day Egypt and Iraq

WHAT WAS IT LIKE?
The oldest game board found to date is the Royal Game of Ur, which dates back to 2600–2400 BCE. According to references in ancient documents, two players competed to race their pieces from one end of the board to another.

GAME SYSTEM:

PLAYING CARDS

EARLIEST KNOWN EXAMPLE:
First referenced in tenth-century Chinese literature

WHERE WAS IT FOUND?
Imperial China

WHAT WAS IT LIKE?
Researchers think that a document about a Chinese princess playing the "leaf game" refers to playing cards. Playing cards first appeared in Europe in the 1300s. The earliest card game known by name was a German game called Karnöffel from 1428.

Games Go Electronic

Now, you might be thinking, an electronic game is a video game, right? That is mostly true today, but many games used electronics before computers and video screens became common. Many of these early electronic games can still be found in arcades. You've probably played a few of them yourself! These "electromechanical games" included pinball machines and "redemption games," such as Skee-Ball and Whac-A-Mole, which tracked points electronically.

At first these games used only mechanical parts: Early pinball machines, for instance, used weighted balls and levers to flip the score counters.

The earliest games to include electronics were not exactly games: They were coin-operated machines that played a song or told your fortune. Some of these early machines incorporated elements of gameplay, such as machines that supposedly tested your strength and lit up when you squeezed a handle or hit a lever. Players generally couldn't control the outcome of these games, and there wasn't always a way to "win"—but people claimed bragging rights for reaching higher levels.

Skee-Ball

The World's First Computer Games

In 1939, the New York World's Fair ushered in the "World of Tomorrow" and introduced the very first computer game. A man named Edward Condon designed the game as part of a technology demonstration for the Westinghouse Corporation. He based the game on a very simple and very ancient game called Nim, in which the person who takes the last counter loses. He called the computer itself the Nimatron. Tens of thousands of people lined up to play the Nimatron. The machine won more than 90% of the time.

Nimatron

While the Nimatron was a huge hit, it was before its time. Computers were still far too expensive for anything other than government or industrial use. Scientists in labs and universities continued to develop new computer programs, but they were used mostly for academic purposes. The public would have to wait years before personal computers made home video games possible. However, the technology primed the imaginations of scientists and programmers who would develop the games that would rocket into the phenomenon we know today.

Early
Computer Games

The history of video games begins with computer gaming. In fact, all video games are really computer games, because all video games are played on some variation on a computer. The difference (and why we use the term "video games" more often) is that games played at the arcade and on consoles have computers built very specifically for gaming and are projected on a TV (that's the "video" part of "video games"), while computer games tend to be played on computers meant for multiple purposes and which display their information on computer monitors. In the early days of computer gaming, which would soon lead to the booming industry of video games we know today, there were very few games, because they were still considered a novelty! Essentially, they were just programs made by computer engineers to show off their machines or to entertain people at special events, and none of them were ever sold. Despite that, these early games paved the way for the video game–dominated world we live in today! Here are some of the very first computer games.

YEAR	GAME	GENRE
1940	*Nim*	The first game, played on a computer called the Nimatron. Designed by Edward Condon for a technology exhibit at the 1939–1940 World's Fair.
1950	*Tic-Tac-Toe*	Played on a computer called Bertie the Brain at the Canadian National Exhibition.
1951	*Nim*	A re-creation of Nim on a new computer, called the Nimrod, for the Festival of Britain.
1952	*OXO (Tic-Tac-Toe)*	Created by A. S. Douglas as part of his PhD thesis for the University of Cambridge. The first game to use graphics on a screen.

YEAR	GAME	GENRE
1955	*Hutspiel*	A serious war game designed by the US military to study different tactical actions in a simulated war between NATO and Soviet forces.
1956	*Checkers*	Arthur Samuel designed the Checkers program for play on an IBM 701 computer. A milestone in artificial intelligence, the program was one of the first "self-learning" games, which improved the more it played. In 1962, it competed on TV against checkers champion Robert Nealey. The computer won.
1958	*NSS Chess Program*	Designed by researchers at Carnegie Mellon University, this game was the first computerized chess game to beat a human player.
1958	*Tennis for Two*	William A. Higinbotham developed this computer game as part of a visitor display for the Brookhaven National Lab in New York. It used a Donner Model 30 analog computer, two aluminum "controller" boxes, and an oscilloscope to display a vertical 2D tennis game. Two players bounced a ball back and forth across the screen, and the machine would make a noise when the ball was hit. Higinbotham designed the game using the computer's ability to plot trajectories. Despite being very popular among lab visitors, it was completely dismantled and used for parts.

Checkers

SPACEWAR!

Gaming's First Big Hit

In 1962, two labs at the Massachusetts Institute of Technology (MIT) in Cambridge held the keys to a video game boom: In the Lincoln Laboratory was the new PDP-1 minicomputer donated by the Digital Equipment Corporation (DEC). In the Artificial Intelligence Laboratory was a young programmer named Steve Russell.

The PDP-1 was smaller, faster, and more interactive than any other computer at the time. During the day, the system was dedicated to official research and university studies, but at night, researchers and students used the computer to create and run their own programs.

Steve Russell was a member of the university's math and electronics club, called the Tech Model Railroad Club (TMRC). The club members called themselves "hackers." The TMRC hackers would meet at the computer lab late at night to create music programs, artificial intelligence routines, and simple games like Tic-Tac-Toe. They were also major fans of science fiction. Combining computer programming with science fiction, Russell and his hacker friends made a game that featured two spaceships that could fly around the screen and shoot torpedoes at each other. The game included accurate space maps and, for that time, state-of-the-art graphics. The result was *Spacewar!*

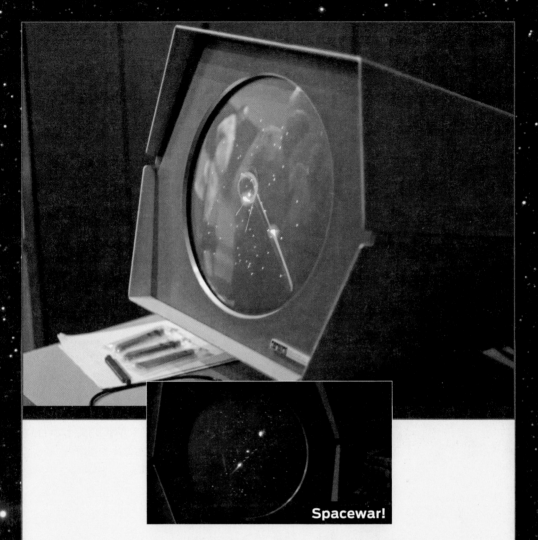

Spacewar!

Spacewar! was one of the first games designed to be played on a minicomputer, and it was designed to be played often and returned to, not deleted. The TMRC hackers quickly got hooked on it, playing often and eventually holding big tournaments. The PDP-1 computer became popular in many university labs, and as users heard about the game, they copied it. The game spread from lab to lab, all over the United States. The game became so popular by the 1970s that the Digital Equipment Corporation decided to include it on every computer they sold. The first true computer game was born!

Despite the success of *Spacewar!,* computers were still very rare and expensive in the 1970s. Not many people outside of university labs and large businesses had a chance to play it. It would take a revolution in computing and a stroke of genius to bring video games to the public. But that was just around the corner.

From Mechanical Coin-Ops to the First Video Game Arcade

The video game craze began in the early 1970s with the invention of two things: the first video arcade machine and the first video game console for the home.

Periscope

In the early 1970s, coin-operated electromechanical machines dominated the arcade world. Games like the 1967 *Periscope* by Sega Enterprises and Chicago Coin's 1968 *Speedway* were longtime favorites. These games had no computer screens and no true animations – players inserted a coin to activate the game and controlled electronic parts that activated lights and sounds.

The first coin-operated video game was created in 1971 by students at Stanford University, and it was designed to run exactly like *Spacewar!* but in a coin-operated machine. They called it *Galaxy Game*. It was a popular game at school, but only one machine was ever made, and it never became a hit in the outside world.

Galaxy Game

Video Games Go Mainstream

The first commercially available, coin-operated video game cabinet, called Computer Space, was essentially a single player version of *Spacewar!* It was invented by Nolan Bushnell, who is now considered one of the founding fathers of the video game industry. In the 1960s, Bushnell, an electrical engineer who had experience working at an amusement park, went to work in Silicon Valley, California. There, he had access to a Stanford University computer lab and its copy of *Spacewar!* Bushnell teamed up with a coworker named Ted Dabney, and together they came up with a special circuit technology, called the transistor-transistor logic circuit, that allowed users to control dots on a TV screen. Using this system, they created *Computer Space*: the first video game to be mass-produced and sold.

The new arcade cabinet marked a major change in gaming: It was the first time the general public could play a video game—it was no longer limited to universities and labs with powerful and expensive computer systems. Unfortunately, *Computer Space* was not a commercial success. Most people found the game's complex controls too technical. The machine was also very expensive to make and hard to sell.

While Bushnell and Dabney's first try at bringing video games to a mass audience was not commercially successful, the experience taught them important lessons about the video game business—from the market to the technology and gameplay—and these lessons would serve them well when they started the Atari Corporation in 1972.

The Brown Box: The First Home Video Game Console

Ralph Baer had been working on ideas for a TV game console since 1951, but they always proved too difficult or costly to make. In 1968, Baer finally came up with a prototype for a video game console that would work with a home TV. Its code name was "The Brown Box." Magnavox Corporation licensed the technology and introduced it in 1972 as the Magnavox Odyssey, the first home video game console available to the public.

By today's standards, the Magnavox Odyssey was surprisingly simple: The actual display was just a few white squares that moved around on a black background to play ball-and-paddle games, such as tennis and hockey. The box included the console, six game cards that unlocked twelve games, two controllers, a user manual, cards, dice, and other paraphernalia. Players would stick plastic overlays onto their TV screens to add different graphics and color to each game.

In its day, however, the Magnavox Odyssey was a marvel. Very few people had ever played a video game before, and TVs had never been interactive. The Odyssey promised to turn the household TV into a source of infinite possibilities and interactive entertainment.

The Magnavox Odyssey was a breakout product: It introduced video games to the general public and opened the door to other ideas in gaming. The Odyssey also defined the basic games and game strategies that would go into the next generation of home video games. The ball-and-paddle design of Odyssey *Tennis* would become the basis of one of the most important successes in video game history.

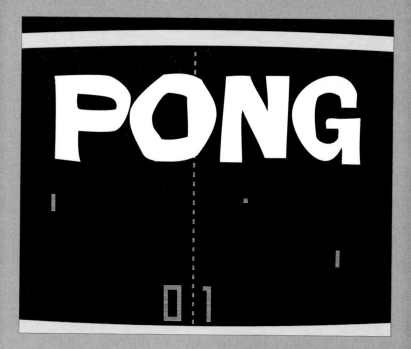

The Game That Started It All

While Magnavox was busy with their Odyssey, Bushnell, Dabney, and another colleague, Alan Alcorn, were working to establish the Atari Corporation. Alcorn was an expert in television electronics and created a version of video table tennis that was very easy to pick up, but also very hard to master. For instance, the speed of the ball increased the longer one played. This element of gameplay—where a high skill level wasn't needed at first, but the difficulty increased later on—was a great leap in video game strategy and capabilities. This idea of increasing skill level and competition became an important factor in video game development and is a key element in almost all successful video games today.

Atari engineered the game as an arcade cabinet and named it *Pong*. The game was an instant success. It was so successful, according to another Atari legend, that once when Alcorn went to repair a broken *Pong* cabinet, he found that the game had stopped working because too many quarters had been slammed into it.

Unfortunately for Atari, *Pong* was easy to copy, and many companies made their own versions. Even that, however, proved two things: People loved *Pong*, and coin-operated video games could be very successful. More massive arcade games soon followed. The arcade revolution was here.

The Golden Age Begins

SCORE<1>   HI-SCORE   SCORE<2>
 0000   0000

The mid 1970s were huge for video game arcades and home consoles. The incredible success of *Pong* and related video games kicked off a whole new industry of video gaming.

Space Invaders

On the arcade side, developers started with the things that made *Pong* so awesome—funny noises, friendly competition, and advancing skill levels—and added new features like improved graphics, steering-wheel controllers, and much more. By 1978, arcade games were everywhere. Then the big one hit: The Japanese company Taito put out a game with a completely new design. Players had to shoot aliens as they fell from the sky and avoid being blasted themselves. It was one of the first games where shooting was the main mechanism. When *Space Invaders* hit the market, people went crazy.

The game was a phenomenon, making $600 million in Japan alone in its first year. People liked *Space Invaders* so much, they dedicated entire arcades to it! Video game arcades became huge moneymaking businesses: Malls and grocery stores installed arcade cabinets, and almost every movie theater had at least a few video games to play.

Consumers and electronics firms were wild about arcade games—and things were going just about the same for the home video game market. After the Magnavox Odyssey, other companies started putting out a wide variety of new consoles. Among them were the 1976 Fairchild Video Entertainment System, which was the first console to use a central processing unit (CPU); the Atari 2600, future king of the consoles; and the Color TV-Game, from a Japanese game manufacturer known as Nintendo.

Fun Fact!

The most popular console of the 1970s and '80s was the Atari 2600. At that time, each game was usually made by a single person! According to game programmer Warren Robinett, "In those old far-off days, each game for the 2600 was done entirely by one person: The programmer . . . conceived the game concept, wrote the program, did the graphics—drawn first on graph paper and converted by hand to hexadecimal—and did the sounds."

Q*Bert

At first, the public was reluctant to invest in home video game consoles. The technology was so new, people didn't know what to expect. But by 1979, the Atari 2600 was the top Christmas gift in America, selling about one million units that year.

Video games had set people's imaginations on fire! By the late 1970s, it seemed everyone wanted to play. Games were improving all the time, and the industry was growing rapidly, laying the groundwork for what would become one of the most exciting and profitable new entertainment industries ever.

Gaming in the Lab:

Top Computer Games Before Home Computers

While arcades and consoles were the dominant video game platforms in the '70s and '80s, computer gaming was still happening—especially in university labs! Smart kids and computer programmers continued to make new games specifically for computer users. These games were run on the most powerful computers in the world, and only students and faculty at these schools had access to these games, meaning computer gaming was a very small club. It also meant that the games that were available were pretty technical, complex (for the time), and heavily focused on strategy and logic.

To see a bit more about some of the earliest hit computer games, take a look at the timeline on pages 20 and 21.

HOT FACT!

While some of the early computer games are pretty rough to play these days due to our modern minds being used to much better graphics and mechanics, some of these early computer games are still a lot of fun to play, and they can often be found online for free! The text-based games like *Zork* and *Adventure* are especially still fun for those who like to read and enjoy a good story, and you'll get pretty much the same exact challenging experience now that they provided to the very first gamers when they were released.

Your greatest challenge lies ahead—and downwards.

ZORK I

INFOCOM

SOFTWARE PUBLISHER
ATARI ST SERIES

INTERACTIVE FICTION

FANTASY

STANDARD LEVEL

The Golden Age of the Arcade:
The Games That Took Over the World

The number of video games available to the public absolutely exploded in the 1980s from a handful to thousands of titles. Now that games were available to the public and designers were getting better and better at making them, video games became the world's biggest, coolest craze, and the charge for that wildly popular trend was led by the games you see in this chapter. Check out our list of the best classic arcade games starting on page 26 of this book!

HOT FACT!

Play these games! As a modern gamer, you have the advantage over kids from the 1980s when it comes to these classic games. Most of them are available online or on modern consoles for very little money, and you only have to pay for them once instead of plugging in quarter after quarter. Even better, most of these games are still tons of fun to play, as this is one of the eras of gaming that has aged quite nicely with its retro graphics and fast-paced gameplay.

Dragon's Lair

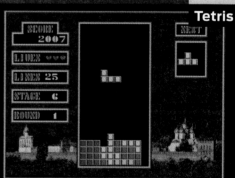

Tetris

Computer Games in

Maze War
An early first-person shooter (FPS) game with 3D graphics. Today, FPS games are among the most popular genres.

Computer Baseball
The first strategy and simulation baseball game for computers—it inspired a whole new genre of sports strategy and simulation games.

Spasim
One of the first multiplayer FPS space games.

1970	1971	1972	1973	1974

Star Trek
Created at the University of California, this was one of the first and most popular *Star Trek* games.

Hunt the Wumpus
Widely considered the first text-based adventure, it was central to the creation of role-playing games, one of the most popular genres today. Gregory Yob developed the game for BASIC, an easily shared and modified programming language. He sold the game through classified listings in computer game magazines.

Airfight
Popular flight simulation game, a genre that would become big in the '90s.

Adventure

A text-based story and puzzle game. One of the most influential games of all time.

Multi-User Dungeon

A revolutionary text-based game that allowed multiple players to interact at the same time. The predecessor of all multiplayer role-playing games, including *World of Warcraft*.

1975 **1976** **1977** **1978** **1979**

Zork/Dungeon

Developed over many years and in many versions, this text-based adventure was technically superior to most other games of its kind. It was released commercially in the early 1980s.

Your greatest challenge lies ahead—and downwards.

INFOCOM

INTERACTIVE FICTION

FANTASY

SOFTWARE FOR YOUR
ATARI ST SERIES

Zork

```
Clearing
You are in a small clearing in a well marked for
east and west.

Canyon View
You are at the top of the Great Canyon on its we
marvelous view of the canyon and parts of the Fr
the canyon, the walls of the White Cliffs join t
Flathead Mountains to the east. Following the Ca
Aragain Falls may be seen, complete with rainbow
flows out from a great dark cavern. To the west
immense forest, stretching for miles around. A p
possible to climb down into the canyon from here.

>down
Rocky Ledge
You are on a ledge about halfway up the wall of the river canyon. You can see
from here that the main flow from Aragain Falls twists along a passage which
it is impossible for you to enter. Below you is the canyon bottom. Above you
is more cliff, which appears climbable.
```

Zork

Gaming in the 1980s:
Consoles Get Better, and Gaming Is Here to Stay

The '80s were the decade when video games became a full-on phenomenon. Games were more colorful, more interactive, and more awesome. No longer limited to computer labs and big businesses, computer games were everywhere, and everyone was in on the fun.

The Golden Age of Arcade Games was in full swing: Machines showcased fancy graphics, new games, and a variety of controls, such as racing wheels. It seemed like every machine offered some new feature. People could see the technology changing right before their eyes. New video game displays offered higher resolutions and brighter colors. Gaming software incorporated artificial intelligence into hundreds of new games. Consoles offered superior sound and gaming experiences, bringing more players to the scene. By 1982, about eight million American households had their own video game console.

The boom in video games was changing the economic landscape. In 1981, the North American video game industry made about $5 billion. In 1982 that number jumped to $8 billion—a 60 percent increase. Compare that with the music and movie industries, which made a combined $7 billion in 1982.

Video games grew from a very small segment of the entertainment industry into the largest segment in just one decade.

The games themselves were having an impact on the culture, too. Many of the characters we now consider icons were born in the 1980s. Consider, for instance, Q*bert, that little dot-eating yellow circle named Pac-Man, and perhaps the most iconic video game character of all, Mario.

Another important change in the video game industry occurred at this time: In 1979, a group of game designers broke off from Atari and started their own company called Activision. This was the first company dedicated to making video game software only—not the machines they were played on. This specialization changed the video game industry and made Activision one of the top game developers in the world. As evidence, see Activision's roster of classic games, including *Pitfall!*, *Tony Hawk's Pro Skater*, *Call of Duty*, *Marvel: Ultimate Alliance*, and the recent hit *Destiny*.

MYTHS from the
Golden Age of the Game Arcades

Video game arcades grew so popular that many myths and legends began spreading like wildfire. Most of these are probably fake, but these tall tales show the impact video games had on the time period.

According to one legend, the Japanese government had to make extra coins one year because so many were sitting in arcade machines!

Many players said they reached scores in the high millions on machines like Defender or Robotron. Some even claimed that they scored so high, the machines broke!

Some people claim to have played an arcade game for more than twenty-four hours straight. They said if they had to eat, they'd eat while playing, and if they had to use the bathroom, they'd find a safe spot for their character to hide in the game or just hope they had enough lives to survive while they were gone.

One legendary story tells of a *Pac-Man* expert who would dazzle less-experienced players by winning every game. (Since the ghosts move in specific patterns and always follow the same rules, players could, theoretically, learn how to win every game. It would be a very impressive feat, if it ever happened!)

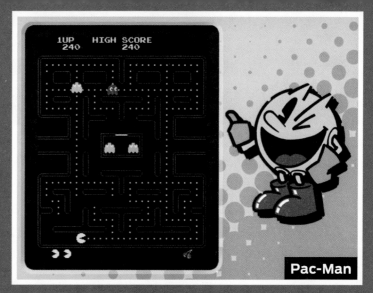

Pac-Man

The game *Frogger* was said to have a "kill screen" that players couldn't get past. This supposedly happened to a whole tournament of players once.

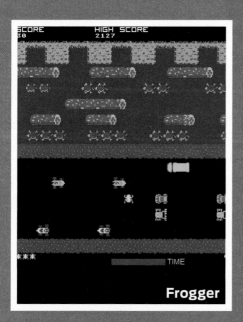

Frogger

According to one story, a boy named Jeffrey R. Yee got a letter from President Ronald Reagan congratulating him for getting a score of 6,131,940 on *Pac-Man*.

The Golden Age of the Arcade: The Games That Took Over the World

The number of video games available to the public absolutely exploded in the 1980s from a handful to thousands of titles. Now that games were available to the public and designers were getting better and better at making them, video games became the world's biggest, coolest craze, and the charge for that wildly popular trend was led by the games you see on this list.

YEAR	GAME	IMPORTANT MILESTONES AND NEAT FACTS
1972	Pong	The first commercial video arcade game.
1976	Breakout	Atari's block-breaking game and Pong descendant, it is still in circulation today.
1978	Space Invaders	The game that started the Golden Age of Arcades.
1979	Galaxian	First game to use RGB color graphics, and Namco's first major hit.
1979	Asteroids	Inspired by the first big game, Spacewar!, this became a video game classic.
1980	Pac-Man	The arcade game so big that it was an international craze all on its own, almost transcending video games. Still a huge cultural icon.
1980	Defender	Side-scrolling space shooter that was important for its beautiful graphics and sound.
1981	Donkey Kong	Nintendo's first hit in the video game world, which revolutionized gaming by giving players a character they could relate to, as well as by founding the "platformer" genre.
1981	Ms. Pac-Man	The video arcade's last megahit.
1982	Pole Position	Made third-person racing games popular.
1982	Q*bert	This game inspired massive amounts of merchandise based on its title character.
1982	Star Trek	The iconic science fiction franchise created by Gene Roddenberry has inspired countless video games, including this popular arcade release by Sega.
1982	Tron	Reality is sometimes stranger than fiction, with a computer game based on a movie about a computer game! Shows gaming's influence on other cultural enterprises.
1983	Dragon's Lair	Used LaserDiscs to create incredible filmlike animation. One of just a few games in the Smithsonian Institution in Washington, DC.

Game: Dragon's Lair

Year: 1983 · Creators: Cinematronics · Genre: Interactive film arcade game

Why it's important: *Dragon's Lair* is a unique piece of video game history. Almost all arcade games, even today, have been heavily focused on fast gameplay and action, but *Dragon's Lair* was all about story and style. The arcade machine actually contained a laser-disc player (an early disc-based film format kind of like a giant CD) that played through an animated fantasy film about a reluctant bumbling hero, and the "gameplay" consisted of players pressing a direction or a button at the right time. It wasn't much in the way of technical action, but it more than made up for it with its stunning full motion video (beautifully hand-drawn) and fun story. Interestingly enough, the gameplay itself isn't very much different from that of games like Telltale's *The Walking Dead* and other adventure games.

HOT FACT!

The animation for *Dragon's Lair* was created by legendary animator Don Bluth, who also drew for the films *The Secret of NIMH*, *An American Tail*, *The Land Before Time*, *All Dogs Go to Heaven*, and *Anastasia*.

The Golden Age of the Arcade: The Games That Took Over the World

HOT FACT!

Play these games! Most of them are available online or on modern consoles for very little money, and you only have to pay for them once instead of plugging in quarter after quarter.

YEAR	GAME	IMPORTANT MILESTONES AND NEAT FACTS
1983	*Mario Bros.*	The arcade game that first made Mario and Luigi the stars, and paved the way for their iconic smash hit on the NES.
1983	*Spy Hunter*	A popular coin-operated arcade game developed by Bally Midway offered players a unique driving experience with technologically advanced car options, superior play value, and a quality sound system. Inspired by popular spy novels and movies, it was the first game to combine driving and shooting at the same time. The experience could be compared with later role-playing games.
1983	*Star Wars*	Digitized the original actors' voices to include in the game, a technique that boosted its popularity and would be used in many other film-related games.
1983	*1942*	The first hit by video game giant Capcom.
1985	*Gauntlet*	An early fantasy-themed arcade game from Atari, it was the first multiplayer dungeon crawl game for arcades.
1987	*Street Fighter*	The first in what would become the series to define fighting games, it also invented many of the features used in such games.
1987	*Double Dragon*	Started another wave of arcade games, this one more violent and real-world focused.
1989	*Tetris*	*Tetris* is one of the most recognizable video games of all time. Designed by Russian engineer Alexey Pajitnov, it was copied by countless developers until Nintendo licensed it in 1989 for the NES and Game Boy. The Nintendo version is now considered definitive. The game's beauty and simplicity is credited with helping ease ordinary people's anxiety about computers.
1989	*Final Fight*	Arguably the last great arcade game of the 1980s, it spawned many sequels.

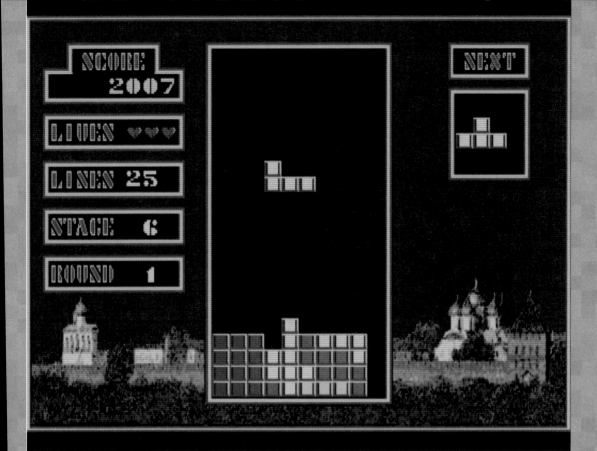

Game: Tetris

Year: 1989 · Creators: Alexey Pajitnov · Genre: Spatial puzzle game

Why it's important: In the argument over what the most popular, best-known video game of all time is, there are only a handful of games that can really contend for the title. Among those is, of course, the game that is not only the best-selling mobile phone game of all time (despite being designed well before mobile phones even had screens), it's also a game that can be found on every single major gaming platform and console. That game is *Tetris*, one of the world's most famous games. Originally, the game was designed by a researcher named Alexey Pajitnov, working in artificial intelligence at the Soviet Academy of Sciences in Moscow, and it was made as a PC game. It spread like wildfire anywhere it was played, jumping from country to country with tremendous speed, with people equally happy to play clones of Pajitnov's game as they were the original. All that mattered were the falling "tetrominos" (a math term describing shapes made of four squares in different combinations) and clearing layers. Since those early days, *Tetris* has remained one of the most common games in the world, and is still a whole lot of fun to play.

The Crash of 1983:
Video Games Face Their First Setback

In 1983, the video game industry faced a disaster. Many companies wanted to cash in on the craze. There were too many different consoles on the market. Bad games were getting produced just to meet demand for new product. Good games were getting copied, or *cloned*, and game manufacturers simply didn't know how to protect their games from cloning. The economic recession in the early '80s peaked in late 1982 and affected spending well into the mid-1980s.

At the same time, home computers were improving and becoming more affordable. A home computer cost about the same as a game console, plus it offered more functionality, such as typing. There were plenty of new computer games to choose from, so many people decided to buy a computer instead of a dedicated game console.

The final straw came from none other than Atari, who put out a very weak console edition of *Pac-Man* and a famously bad game based on the movie *E.T.* The games sold so poorly that Atari had to discard thousands of game cartridges.

When the market finally crashed, nearly all North American video game companies failed. Magnavox and Coleco stopped making games and consoles entirely. Many software publishers went out of business. Even Atari went bankrupt. Over the next two years, video game sales continued to fall. Before the crash in 1983, video game sales in North America were about $3.2 billion; by 1985, they were just $100 million.

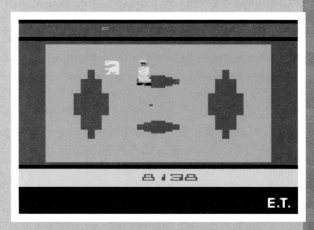

E.T.

```
>s
Clearing
You are in a small clearing in a well marked forest path that extends to the
east and west.

>e
Canyon View
You are at the top of the Great Canyon on its west wall. From here there is a
marvelous view of the canyon and parts of the Frigid River upstream. Across
the canyon, the walls of the White Cliffs join the mighty ramparts of the
Flathead Mountains to the east. Following the Canyon upstream to the north,
Aragain Falls may be seen, complete with rainbow. The mighty Frigid River
flows out from a great dark cavern. To the west and south can be seen an
immense forest, stretching for miles around. A path leads northwest. It is
possible to climb down into the canyon from here.

>down
Rocky Ledge
You are on a ledge about halfway up the wall of the river canyon. You can see
from here that the main flow from Aragain Falls twists along a passage which
it is impossible for you to enter. Below you is the canyon bottom. Above you
is more cliff, which appears climbable.
```

Zork | **Quest for Glory**

Quest for Glory I   [score 16 of 500]

"Help me, Brave and Kind Hero."

The Growth of Computer Gaming

In 1983, home computers were becoming more powerful and less expensive. They had better graphics and offered more functionality than video game consoles—and there were plenty of games to play.

Games like *Zork* and *The Hobbit* were popular text-based adventure games. Real-life simulation games were also popular, such as *Flight Simulator*, Microsoft's first computer game for the home user.

The fact that computers were useful in other ways besides gaming made them more practical for families. Computers were often more powerful than consoles, so they could support more complex games. Also, computers often had a modular design, so users could upgrade or add new devices without having to buy a whole new system. The move toward computer games also expanded the range of games and users who played them. Adults, for example, were more likely to own a computer than a game console. This led to the creation of more serious games with adult themes, complex stories, and more difficult strategies—game genres that are still very popular today.

The adventure game—sometimes called a point-and-click game—was one of these new genres. In an adventure game, players would control characters, solving puzzles and interacting with other characters along the way. These games typically involved very little combat. Many of the games now considered masterpieces of the adventure genre came from two companies: Sierra and LucasArts, the gaming branch of Lucasfilm, creators of the *Star Wars* and *Indiana Jones* games.

The most significant event of the 1980s was the advent of online gaming. Players used dial-up phone-line modems to connect to electronic bulletin boards, where they could connect and play games with other players. Early games were text-based—such as multi-user dungeon games—but by the end of the 1980s some used graphics for online play. While these early games were fairly simple, they were very popular with gamers, and would lead to today's massive multiplayer online games, such as *Everquest* and *World of Warcraft*.

Computers Come to the Home
Major Computer Games of the 1980s

With home computers growing in power massively during the 1980s, games on the computer were by far the most complex and graphically beautiful of the era, though they were not as insanely popular as arcade machines due to computers still being pretty expensive. Despite that, computers were starting to reach more and more homes around the world, and an industry to create games for these machines grew up around the new trend of home computing. These are the best games of the era, as well as games that are important to video game history for inventing genres and being the ancestors of the most popular games of today.

SimCity

YEAR	GAME	GENRE	WHAT MAKES IT AWESOME
1980	*Rogue*	Procedurally generated dungeon crawler	One of the first games to use procedurally generated maps and adventures, meaning they were different every time you played. Spawned the "Roguelike" subgenre.
1980–1989	*Microsoft Flight Simulator series*	Flight simulator	Microsoft's first foray into gaming and the first major flight simulator.
1981–1989	*Ultima I–V*	Role-play game	One of the most influential role-playing series of all time; spawned countless sequels and imitators
1982–1989	*Sierra adventures: King's Quest, Quest for Glory, Space Quest, Police Quest, Leisure Suit Larry*	Graphic adventure/ point-and-click	Sierra Entertainment pioneered the popular and influential adventure game genre, which focused on story, character, and complex puzzles instead of combat or arcade gaming.
1983	*Boulder Dash*	Arcade-style puzzle platformer	Game that focused on puzzles rather than graphics. It was favored for its depth of content.
1983	*Lode Runner*	Arcade-style puzzle platformer	Popular sci-fi puzzle game that included one of the first level editors in gaming.

YEAR	GAME	GENRE	WHAT MAKES IT AWESOME
1984	*Sabre Wulf*	Arcade maze	Beautiful bright graphics that are still striking, in a complex maze game with a solid story and setting.
1984	*Elite*	Space combat simulator	Undeniably the most important space combat simulator of its day. It took space combat more seriously than arcade games and defined the genre. Elite continues to develop games today.
1984-1989	LucasArts games: *Ballblazer, Habitat, Maniac Mansion, Zak McKracken and the Alien Mindbenders, Indiana Jones and the Last Crusade*	Variety, including action, graphic adventure/point-and-click, and flight/historical simulator	In the 1980s, LucasArts trounced every competitor in whatever genre it entered, although their best games were arguably point-and-click adventure games. The company made a point of including a lot of pop culture and irreverent humor in its games, something few companies had done before.
1985	*The Oregon Trail*	Strategy/simulator	A favorite among kids, it became an icon in the minds of millions.
1985	*Paradroid*	Shoot-'em-up/puzzle	One of the best-rated games of the decade. A sci-fi puzzle classic!
1985	*Where in the World Is Carmen Sandiego*	Trivia/adventure	Parents saw this game as educational, making it a bestseller. The game was so popular, it spawned a board game, TV shows, and sequels.
1985	*F-15 Strike Eagle*	Flight combat simulator	Like *Elite* but for a real plane. This game took air combat seriously and sold millions of copies.
1986	*Trade Wars 2002*	Resource gathering	A complex strategy game. One of the first successful online multiplayer games.
1987	*Sid Meier's Pirates*	Action-adventure/strategy	The first game to include the name "Sid Meier's," this title simulated the life of a pirate, with fencing, ship combat, and diplomacy.
1987	*Dungeon Master*	Dungeon crawler/role-playing game	Introduced many important RPG elements, but particularly was an early real-time RPG, instead of the common turn-based.
1988	*Wasteland*	Role-play/tactical combat	One of the best-realized role-playing games of all time. One of the few successful non-fantasy games in the genre.
1988	*Battle Chess*	Chess simulation	Best known for the fun it added to the classic game, with animated figures that battled each other on screen.
1989	*Populous*	God game/real-time strategy	Considered the first "god game," in which a player acts as the deity. The game's creator, Peter Molyneux, is considered the father of the genre.
1989	*Prince of Persia*	Action-adventure	The first in a long-lasting and genre-spanning series, it featured incredible animation, complex battle scenes, and an engaging story.
1989	*SimCity*	City building	The game that brought the world nearly limitless Sim games, including *The Sims*. It inspired more "build a city and make it run" games, like *Rollercoaster Tycoon, Caesar,* and more.

The Rise of Nintendo

In 1985, many people thought the video game boom was over. However, one console manufacturer managed to stay alive during the crash—and thrive—primarily because it was located in Japan, not America.

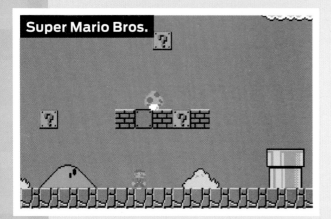
Super Mario Bros.

The Nintendo Entertainment System (NES) was revolutionary in every way: It was faster and more powerful. It had better, 16-bit graphics and more accurate and sturdy controllers. It could do new things and was a sleeker-looking product. The NES also had high-quality, fully vetted, and exclusive games. One of those games was *Super Mario Bros.*, which would become the must-play game of the day.

DiD YOU KNOW? Nintendo's console was called **Famicom** in Japan and the **Nintendo Entertainment System** (NES) in America.

By 1988, US sales of Nintendo games were greater than all PC software sales combined. In that year alone, Nintendo sold about 7 million NES systems.

In 1989, Nintendo released the Game Boy, the world's first portable video game system. It became clear: Nintendo was now king of all things gaming. The company had brought the console market back in a huge way, and set itself up as the industry leader, setting the ground rules for all game companies to come.

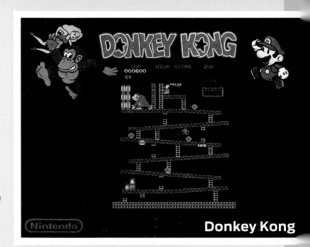
Donkey Kong

The Story of Shigeru Miyamoto

Shigeru Miyamoto stumbled into game design. He received his degree in industrial design and then landed a job at Nintendo after his father got him an interview at the company. Miyamoto designed the company's first arcade title, *Radar Scope*. He was also their first artist, and worked on other early arcade games like *Sheriff*.

Radar Scope wasn't a big success, so Nintendo asked Miyamoto to repurpose the existing arcade cabinets for a new game. According to Miyamoto, "No one else was available." But what Miyamoto did with the opportunity changed the face of gaming.

Using classic *Popeye* characters as inspiration, Miyamoto created a game that featured a girl captured by a gorilla. In the game, a carpenter named Jumpman had to dodge barrels and climb ladders to rescue the girl. The game was called *Donkey Kong*, and it was Miyamoto's first hit for Nintendo. In fact, Miyamoto created most of Nintendo's early success stories, including *Super Mario Bros.* and *The Legend of Zelda*.

Miyamoto's idea that games should have storylines and characters changed the face of gaming. Much of his inspiration came from memories of childhood adventures. In his youth, Miyamoto enjoyed looking at nature, climbing hills, exploring caves, and playing in the countryside. Combining his childhood love for nature and exploration with his technical know-how, Miyamoto created some of the most well-known and well-loved games in the world. His work also helped make Nintendo one of the most important companies in the history of video games.

Nintendo & Sega Face Off

Nintendo wasn't the only console maker in the '90s. Other companies, such as Casio and Commodore, tried to get in on the fun, too. Other competitors included the Sega SG-1000, which was only available in Japan, and the newest system from Atari, the 7600. But the competition was not even close for these third-generation companies. Nintendo ruled the roost.

Sega tried to narrow the difference for the fourth generation of systems. Sega went on an all-out campaign to be the cooler, edgier console, with a sleek black machine called the Genesis. Nintendo was focused on creating games for all ages, so Sega stepped in with a console for a different age group and personality type. They were so committed to this idea of being the anti-Nintendo that they released a series of commercials with the tagline "Genesis does what Nintendon't!"

In addition to that catchy slogan, Sega added an edgy character to its arsenal of new games: the fast-moving, spiky-haired Sonic the Hedgehog. Compared with Nintendo's Mario—who was a bit round, a little slow, and always friendly—Sonic almost flew off the screen. Sonic also had an irreverent attitude that Sega hoped would appeal to kids who liked *The Simpsons* and *Teenage Mutant Ninja Turtles.*

The strategy worked: Sega sold millions of units of *Sonic the Hedgehog,* coming in a close second to Nintendo's *Super Mario World.*

While Sega sold about 30 million units of its Genesis console —a healthy number by any account—Nintendo's new Super NES moved nearly 50 million units worldwide. So although Sega caught up, there was still no doubt which company was the industry leader in consoles.

Gaming Goes Mobile

The 1990s also saw the rise of Nintendo's Game Boy, the first complete handheld gaming system, introduced in the US in 1989. Now gamers could bring their favorite Nintendo titles with them everywhere! Other companies such as Neo Geo and Sega would release their own handheld gaming devices. But with new, enhanced versions coming out every few years, the Game Boy was never knocked off its top spot. Its descendant, the Nintendo DS, is still one of the most successful systems of all time.

There is no question that Nintendo was the reigning video game champion in the '90s, and Mario was the biggest mascot since Pac-Man, a title he still holds today.

Arcade Games Pop Back Up

After the fall of arcade games in the '80s, there was a surprising comeback in the '90s. A surge of new arcade titles revitalized arcade gaming.

Street Fighter II

The resurgence started with the release of *Street Fighter II,* a game that took the basic combat of *Street Fighter* and added better graphics, wild combination moves, and special abilities. It also changed the focus of the game from just two fighters to a whole cast of characters fighting all over the world. This game was more than successful—it has defined the fighting genre ever since. In fact, the *Street Fighter* formula is still the primary style used on the competitive e-sports fighting circuit, which holds massive competitions.

Mortal Kombat

Mortal Kombat followed *Street Fighter*'s karate-kicking footsteps, but added a new element of violence to the game. *Mortal Kombat* used real, costumed actors and photo-capture technology to depict more graphic violence. The game was immensely popular, but controversial for many parents who did not want their kids playing violent games. Many spoke out in favor of new regulations on games.

NBA Jam

Increased action defined other arcade games, too. Sports games, such as *NBA Jam*, became very action heavy and encouraged intense competition for multiple players. Another new game feature first introduced in arcade games was polygonal 3D graphics. Cabinets for enhanced 3D games, such as *Virtua Fighter* and *Tekken*, had to be equipped with high-powered computers to run the new technology.

Arcade Games — Here to Stay

It wasn't long before game consoles and home computers caught up and surpassed arcades in terms of graphics, and most big arcade games were ported to consoles anyway. This didn't spell the end for arcades, though: It forced them to innovate. The next generation of arcade games included high-end controllers and devices that simply weren't available for home use. Games like *Area 51* and *The House of the Dead* incorporated new 3D graphics and light guns that were much more advanced than anything available for a home console. Other titles, such as *Time Crisis* and *Dance Dance Revolution*, went even further by incorporating pedals or pads that could be activated with the feet.

The most advanced arcade games offered unique competitive experiences or technology that was not available for consoles. Today's arcade games still contain the most up-to-date technology in the video game industry.

Area 51

The House of the Dead

Time Crisis

Dance Dance Revolution

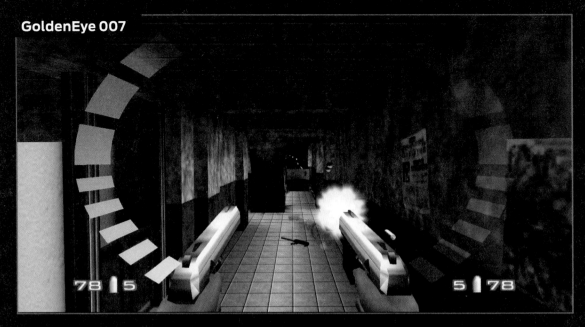

3D Graphics Emerge: The Beginning of Modern Gaming

Gamers still enjoy playing *Pong* and *Spacewar!* online, and many classic games for the NES and Genesis are available for newer systems through re-releases. But modern gaming has come a long way and only consoles from the fifth generation onward resemble today's games. Features such as 3D graphics, specialized controllers, and high-impact gameplay weren't available on consoles until the 32/64-bit era.

The graphics on fifth-generation machines were four times more powerful than those of the fourth generation, which only had 16 bits to work with. The new graphics were mind blowing to people in the '90s. Up until then, nearly all 3D was false 3D, having been developed with wireframe graphics. Some early disc-based consoles featured full-motion video. However, these movies had limited interactivity.

The first console to successfully integrate 3D graphics and mark the fifth-generation of modern gaming was the PlayStation. It used a new controller design, 64-bit graphics, and a fancy new CD drive instead of cartridges to provide an entirely new kind of gaming experience. It allowed home users to experience advanced 3D graphics, and people loved it.

Crash Bandicoot

LAP 2/3   TIME 01'23"80

MARIO STAR   Luigi's

Mario Kart

Tomb Raider

41

PlayStation

The PlayStation was released in Japan in December 1994 and in North America nine months later. It was an immediate hit, selling two million units six months after its release in Japan. In America, it boasted the most modern games available for every genre.

Games for the PlayStation ranged from family friendly to edgy, from fast action to strategic. Among the most popular were *Crash Bandicoot*, *Spyro the Dragon*, *Battle Arena Toshinden*, *Ridge Racer*, *Metal Gear Solid*, and *MechWarrior 2*.

While other game systems offered games that were adapted from different platforms, many PlayStation titles were entirely new. For instance, *Metal Gear Solid* was a revelation in the stealth combat genre. It was inventive, challenging, and full of mature themes. The characters and setting looked like no other. *Tomb Raider* was another game that didn't shy away from violent combat scenes or difficult puzzles. The main character was a gun-toting, bad-guy-wrecking woman—and she looked like a fairly realistic woman, too! The *Tony Hawk* series brought extreme sports and crazy tricks to the masses. Times were changing!

GAME ON!

Though the PlayStation dominated the fifth generation, and the Nintendo 64 was its only real competition, there were actually many other consoles released in the '90s. Some gaming publications predicted that there would be another market crash like in 1983. Luckily, it didn't happen!

Nintendo 64

For a while, it seemed like the PlayStation was going to be the only successful console of the mid-to-late '90s, but it's never a good idea to count out the good folks at Nintendo. Setbacks in design delayed Nintendo's fifth-generation entry into the US market, but in 1996 the Nintendo 64 was released.

In contrast to the sleek, two-pronged controller for the PlayStation, the Nintendo 64 had an unusual three-pronged controller with a D-pad on the left, thumb stick in the middle, and buttons on the right. The boxy PlayStation was mostly gray and black, but the Nintendo 64 had more curves and more colorful, kid-friendly buttons.

Despite the less sophisticated look, the 64's cartridge system was technically much faster than the PlayStation. However, the PlayStation's CDs could hold more data, allowing it to play more complex games. It was hard to decide which system was better.

But Nintendo knew how to make games, and the company released a series of games that included some of the best titles in video game history: *Super Mario 64*, *Yoshi's Story*, *Mario Kart 64*, *Mario Party*, *Super Smash Bros.*, *Mario Tennis*, *Mario Golf*, and two *Legend of Zelda* titles, *Majora's Mask* and *Ocarina of Time*. The company also included some more sophisticated sports and adult titles, such as the *Turok* series, the popular *Goldeneye 007*, *1080° Snowboarding*, and even a few *Mortal Kombat* games.

In the end, Nintendo's late start and the public's clamoring for things that felt modern and edgy meant that the PlayStation outsold the N64 and, in some ways, won the decade in the console wars.

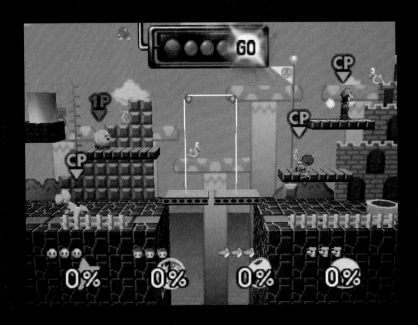

Major Trends Evolve

The '90s were a period of great innovation in gaming. New technology, the expansion of the industry, and new tastes and attitudes helped fuel what was one of the more volatile periods in gaming history. Here are a few of the biggest trends and changes in gaming from the 1990s that still apply today:

New tech, better tech. From the NES to the PlayStation, and from 3D to disc drives to new controller feedback, technology drove the gaming boom of the '90s.

Bigger budgets, bigger games, more Hollywood. Design budgets skyrocketed and creation teams expanded. Popular musicians and actors were brought in to work on games and every part of game design became more attractive and fun to play.

Violence and mature themes became more common. People who had grown up with arcades and video games were now adults, and they were interested in more sophisticated content. Some developers stopped making children's games altogether, focusing instead on these more mature games.

Spyro the Dragon

CAMERA
AP SENSR
CIGS
NONE

NONE

Metal Gear Solid

Resident Evil

It's All About Control(lers)

One piece of tech that changed thoroughly at this time and, in the process, changed gaming on a fundamental level was the controller.

Long gone were the days of awkward controllers with strange knobs and weird patterns of buttons. Starting with the NES and Sega Genesis, controllers became easier to hold (more "ergonomic" is the term), sturdier, and started featuring an array of new, useful buttons. This opened up console games to being much more complicated automatically, bringing the console closer to the level of the depth of PC games.

Still, even the original PlayStation's controller is somewhat foreign to the modern gamer, because up until the PlayStation Dual Analog Controller (released in 1997), no major console used the standard "two thumbstick" controller variation. The thumbstick we know and love, and which also goes by the name "analog stick," has actually been around since the 1970s with a series of consoles known as the Prinztronic/Acetronic/Interton consoles, and they were used for various specialty and rare consoles over the next two decades. It wasn't until PlayStation decided to take some tech they'd built for a large controller used for flight simulators and turn it into a smaller regular controller that the two-thumbstick controller hit major consoles.

Ever since then, it's been the standard in just about every major console. This even includes Nintendo, which has offered a dual analog controller for every console since the GameCube.

Dual Analog Controller

Violent Video Games and the ESRB

Games did not have content ratings before the 1990s. However, public outcry about violence in games such as *Mortal Kombat* led the US Congress to hold hearings on the topic. These hearings were, interestingly enough, often focused on the fact that the games *Mortal Kombat* and *Night Trap* didn't just show violence with computer graphics, they also included full-motion video captures of actors engaging in violence. This was considered to be a bigger issue than if the characters had just been hand-drawn.

The debates over violence in games and how it should be handled was intense, with both members of Congress and the video game companies themselves all taking different stances on the issue. Eventually, many of the major game companies banded together to create an organization to develop a universal games-ratings system. This was founded in 1994 as the Interactive Digital Software Association, and it was created by these companies because they feared letting Congress create their own organization without input from designers. Not long after, this organization became the ESRB that we know today.

The Growth of PC Gaming

Like consoles, personal computers were becoming more powerful all the time. However, computers had one major advantage over consoles: They could be upgraded. They also had different input tools, such as keyboards and mouse devices, that allowed for more complex inputs and more precise control. These two factors allowed for different types of games to be developed for the PC.

Half-Life

FIRST-PERSON SHOOTER & COMBAT

First-person shooter and combat games were big genres for the PC. Games such as *Wolfenstein 3D*, *Doom*, and *Quake* were very popular and became more complex with enhanced graphics and plotlines. The 1998 release of *Half-Life*, a sci-fi FPS that broke ground with its story, physics, and shooting mechanics, brought two multiplayer-only expansions with it, *Counter-Strike* and *Team Fortress Classic*. Sequels of those games are among the top-played PC games today.

King's Quest V

ADVENTURE OR POINT-AND-CLICK

Notable examples of this include *Day of the Tentacle*, the *Monkey Island* series, *Indiana Jones and the Fate of Atlantis*, *The Dig*, *Loom*, *Quest for Glory III*, and *King's Quest V*, among others. With real voice acting, whip-smart scripts, and artists who made every scene look like a painting, this genre turned out video game masterpieces in the 1990s.

Daggerfall

ROLE-PLAYING

Role-playing games were not exclusively about online play at this time, either. Current games like *Fallout 4*, *Skyrim*, *Diablo III*, and *The Witcher 3* owe a huge debt to the pioneering role-playing games of the 1990s. In fact, the original *Diablo* came out in 1996. Companies such as BioWare, Interplay, and Black Isle mastered the top-down role-playing style in *Fallout*, *Fallout 2*, and the *Baldur's Gate* and *Icewind Dale* series. *Skyrim* is a descendant of *The Elder Scrolls*, *Arena*, and *Daggerfall*, all big hits in the '90s. Like many genres, modern role-playing games owe quite a lot to this time.

Dune II

REAL-TIME STRATEGY

The real-time strategy game, or RTS, was also invented in the 1990s. The RTS genre was important because it led to two of today's most popular games: *League of Legends* and *Dota 2*. Prior to this, most strategy games were turn-based, meaning time had to be advanced manually. By the 1990s, computers were powerful enough to synchronize the player's actions with the game simulation. The first game of this kind was *Herzog Zwei*, a European mech-command game released in 1990, but it was *Dune II* that made the format popular. Being able to control resources, individual units, and complex bases made *Dune II* a hit and led to the creation of now-classic games like *Age of Empires*, *StarCraft*, *Command and Conquer*, and *Warcraft*.

Ultima Online

MASSIVE MULTIPLAYER ONLINE ROLE-PLAYING GAME (MMORPG)

The first true, massive online gaming communities started growing in the PC world at this time. The most popular multi-user games were first-person shooters and role-playing games, such as dungeon crawlers. Faster Internet connections and powerful computers made sophisticated graphics-based multiplayer games possible. Among the most popular of the massively multiplayer online role-playing games were *Meridian 59* and *The Realm Online. Ultima Online* had thousands of players creating complex virtual lives in a fantasy setting in which they could do everything from building a house to slaying dragons. In 1999, a game called *Everquest* became the first online gaming community with hundreds of thousands of subscribers playing at once. In the 2000s, this genre would come to dominate PC gaming.

The Sims

TURN-BASED

Turn-based games like *Civilization* and sim games like Maxis's *Sim* series were also popular in the 1990s, while the Internet and software such as Java and Flash made it possible to create simple, inexpensive games for people to play from anywhere.

Iconic Games from the '80s and '90s: The Most Important and Most Awesome

If you're looking for some new games as well as some of the best games from history that are still totally a blast to play, make a beeline for the games on these lists. These games are mostly pre-3D but still look incredible because this is when pixel artists were the best they'd ever been (and may ever be again). These games aren't quite as complicated as the ones we have today, but they are also way beyond the arcade and the early days of gaming in terms of fun and complexity. Try a few, and we promise you'll find at least one or two new favorites if not one or two dozen.

YEAR	GAME	WHAT MAKES IT AWESOME
1985- 1990	*Super Mario Bros. series* CONSOLE: NES GENRE: Platformer	One of the most iconic games of all time, the first has sold over forty million copies and spawned several successful sequels.
1986	*The Legend of Zelda* CONSOLE: Famicom, then NES GENRE: Action-adventure	The first in the massively popular, long-lasting series.
1986	*Metroid* CONSOLE: Famicom, then NES GENRE: Action-adventure	One of the first games to make the lead role a female, especially in action games. The player had to complete the whole game in less than five hours to find this out.
1987	*Metal Gear* CONSOLE: MSX2 computer, NES GENRE: Stealth	The game that created the stealth genre.
1987- current	*Final Fantasy series* CONSOLE: NES, SNES, PlayStation GENRE: JRPG	The definitive Japanese role-playing game series, which continues to be the most popular of its kind today.
1988	*Mega Man 2* CONSOLE: NES GENRE: Platformer/shooter	Fun fact about this game is that the original box art shows Mega Man with a pistol, a weapon he does not have in the game.
1989	*Phantasy Star II* CONSOLE: Sega Genesis GENRE: RPG	One of the most iconic games of all time, the first has sold over forty million copies and spawned several successful sequels.

Fight
Tools
Item

EDGAR	195
LOCKE	194
TERRA	110

Final Fantasy VI

Game: the Final Fantasy series

Year: 1987-current · Creators: Square Enix
Genre: Japanese Role-Playing Game/Other (for spin-offs)

Why it's important: *Final Fantasy* is beloved in a way that few other series are. With very close to 30 years' worth of games now released in the Final Fantasy multiverse (because there is not just one or two universes in the series, but many), there's so much content in the *Final Fantasy* series in terms of characters, settings, plots, and more that it's hard to summarize it all. Basically, though, the games are set in massive, detailed worlds and the core games (about 15 or so) as well as some of the spin-offs are the poster titles for the Japanese role-playing game genre, utilizing turn-based team combat and exploration of very large worlds with many complex settings and plots. These games are often rich in beautiful details and require dozens if not hundreds of hours of deeply tactical gameplay to beat. They often provide many different ways to play through a central story with a staggering number of plots, subplots, and characters. Don't be too overwhelmed to try one out, though: These games are masterful at drawing you into their stories and gameplay, and there's a reason that *Final Fantasy* is one of the most popular series of all time.

Final Fantasy II

Tortoise 2	Rydia	444/ 444
BlackLiz 2	Rosa	698/ 698
	Cecil	1196/1196
	Yang	1321/1321
	Kain	1026/1026

HOT FACT!

As one of the most popular and long-lasting series of all time, there are now over 70 different video games in the *Final Fantasy* brand! Wow!

Iconic Video Games from the '80s and '90s: The Most Important and Most Awesome

YEAR	GAME	WHAT MAKES IT AWESOME
1990	*John Madden Football* CONSOLE: Sega Genesis GENRE: Sports	The most successful in what became the series that would define football games.
1991	*The Legend of Zelda: A Link to the Past* CONSOLE: SNES GENRE: Action-adventure	Though it's the third game in the *Zelda* franchise, this one is where many of the major elements of the series come in, like the ultra-famous Master Sword. This game repeatedly makes it into lists of the top 100 and even 25 games of all time for its balanced gameplay and beautiful pixelated graphics.
1991	*Sonic the Hedgehog* CONSOLE: Sega Genesis GENRE: Platformer	The only character to rival those of Nintendo in popularity in the 1990s.
1992	*NHLPA Hockey '93* CONSOLE: SNES GENRE: Sports	One of the best-loved sports games of all time.
1993	*FIFA International Soccer* CONSOLE: All systems, including PC GENRE: Sports	The first game in the bestselling FIFA franchise.
1993	*Kirby's Adventure* CONSOLE: NES GENRE: Platformer	One of Nintendo's other iconic characters.
1994	*Super Metroid* CONSOLE: SNES GENRE: Action-adventure/platformer	Even more popular than the original.
1994	*Donkey Kong Country* CONSOLE: SNES GENRE: Platformer	Revolutionary 3D-rendered graphics helped the SNES continue to compete against the newly released PlayStation.

ST 4:03
BSN

DET 1
PIT 0

Game: NHLPA Hockey '93

Year: 1992 · Creators: Park Place Productions · Genre: Sports

Why it's important: If you've played a sports game lately, you know that they are getting closer and closer every year to simulating a real-life sporting event with 100 percent accuracy. What you might not know, however, is just how completely unlike real sports the original sports games were (remember, *Pong* was once considered very close to actual tennis). Making sports games more real, complex, and heavily strategic was an endeavor that *NHLPA Hockey '93* took as its mission, and it was considered hugely successful. By adding real players into the game with abilities based on their real-world selves, and by making the game more about how you could use those abilities correctly in a strategic way to win instead of just button-mashing, *NHLPA Hockey '93* helped to bring sports games out of the pure action arcade realm and into the strategic simulation style we know and love in this generation of gaming.

HOT FACT!

Interestingly, this game got a license to use National Hockey League player names from the NHL Player's Association, but it didn't get the license from the NHL itself for the team names. Though there are no team logos or names, each team is named by its location and given its team colors and correct players.

Iconic Video Games from the '80s and '90s: The Most Important and Most Awesome

YEAR	GAME	WHAT MAKES IT AWESOME
1994	*The Need for Speed* CONSOLE: 3DO GENRE: Racing	First title of one of the definitive racing game series.
1994-1998	*Tekken series* CONSOLE: PlayStation, arcade GENRE: Fighting	The definitive fighting games of the decade.
1995	*Chrono Trigger* CONSOLE: SNES GENRE: RPG	Highly praised for its multiple endings and side quests in a very complex plot.
1996	*Tomb Raider* CONSOLE: PlayStation GENRE: Action-adventure/platformer	Featured a strong female lead and amped-up violence; one of the most popular games of the decade.
1996	*Pokémon Red and Blue versions* CONSOLE: Game Boy GENRE: RPG/Tactical combat	The first two games in the second most popular game series of all time; started a craze that is still going strong today.
1996	*PaRappa the Rapper* CONSOLE: PlayStation GENRE: Rhythm	Before *Dance Dance Revolution* and *Guitar Hero*, *PaRappa the Rapper* was one of the earliest examples of a major console rhythm game that became a huge hit.
1996	*Super Mario 64* CONSOLE: Nintendo 64 GENRE: Platformer	The bestselling game of the generation and Mario's venture into 3D. The Nintendo 64 controller was designed for this game.
1996	*Resident Evil* CONSOLE: PlayStation, Sega Saturn GENRE: Survival horror	The game that caused survival and horror games to explode.
1996	*Crash Bandicoot* CONSOLE: PlayStation GENRE: Platfomer	PlayStation's answer to Mario and Sonic.

Game: The Need for Speed

Year: 1994 · Creators: Pioneer Productions/Electronic Arts Canada
Genre: Racing

Why it's important: The first in a series of racing games that stretches over 25 titles all the way from 1994 to the current day, *The Need for Speed* was an attempt to make a popular and approachable car racing game that used cars that behaved like the actual cars do in the real world. These cars were the stars of *The Need for Speed*; also included were lots of images and footage of the cars in real life. This proved to be a big draw for car lovers all over the world. This attention to real-world detail paired with fun but very challenging gameplay and (for the first time) an extensive number of tracks to race on made the game a massive hit. So massive, in fact, that it forced all other racing games to take notice of what it did, and indeed it has spawned many sequels, and even games from other developers.

HOT FACT!

To really nail the accuracy when it came to representing the cars in *The Need for Speed*, the developers worked with the car magazine *Road & Track* to get the virtual cars as close to the real cars as possible. Each car even makes realistic sounds in the game!

Iconic Games from the '80s and '90s: The Most Important and Most Awesome

YEAR	GAME	WHAT MAKES IT AWESOME
1997	*GoldenEye 007* CONSOLE: Nintendo 64 GENRE: First-person shooter	Considered by many to be a highlight of '90s shooter gaming.
1997	*Castlevania: Symphony of the Night* CONSOLE: PlayStation, Sega Saturn GENRE: Action-adventure/platformer	The *Castlevania* games took the action platformer and made it more adult, both for being darker and for being more difficult.
1997	*Gran Turismo* CONSOLE: PlayStation GENRE: Racing	The bestselling game on PlayStation, it sold 10.8 million copies.
1997	*Star Fox 64* CONSOLE: Nintendo 64 GENRE: On-rails shooter	The first 3D polygon game by Nintendo, and only their second-ever game to use 3D graphics at all.
1998	*Spyro the Dragon* CONSOLE: PlayStation GENRE: Platformer	One of the original hit PlayStation series, *Spyro* was meant to be a game in the vein of the Nintendo 3D platformers that expanded on the genre by using the superior capabilities of the PlayStation's technology.
1998	*The Legend of Zelda: Ocarina of Time* CONSOLE: Nintendo 64 GENRE: Action-adventure	Considered by some to be the best of all *Zelda* games.
1998	*Metal Gear Solid* CONSOLE: PlayStation GENRE: Stealth	Took the *Metal Gear* formula and put it in 3D; considered one of the best games of all time.
1999	*Tony Hawk's Pro Skater* CONSOLE: PlayStation GENRE: Extreme sports	Popularized the extreme sports genre almost overnight.
1999	*Super Smash Bros.* CONSOLE: Nintendo 64 GENRE: Fighting	Nintendo's take on the fighting game, with most of their popular characters.

Game: Tony Hawk's Pro Skater

Year: 1999 · Creators: Aaron Cammarata/Chris Rausch
(Neversoft, many other developers for console ports) · Genre: Extreme sports

Why it's important: The late 1990s was the perfect time to release a video game featuring extreme sports, as they were getting pretty darn huge all over the world, and the man leading the charge was the legendary pro skater Tony Hawk. The game released using Hawk's name could easily have been a simple arcade game, with few moves and basic gameplay, but *Tony Hawk's Pro Skater* went above and beyond to try to create the most fun, mind-blowing (at the time) game by incorporating hundreds of moves, an extreme degree of control, a detailed and realistic physics system, and an attitude and feeling that completely matched that of the real sport of skating. This game was praised as one of the best of its era, and if you were a gamer at the time, you remember how hard it was to even find a copy! Since this game, the extreme sports genre has become one of the staples of video games, and all titles since *Tony Hawk's Pro Skater* owe much to this groundbreaking game.

HOT FACT!

Tony Hawk's performance at the 1998 X Games event in San Diego, California, where he took home a Bronze and a Gold medal, helped him to land the deal for this iconic game.

Standout Games from the Golden Age of the PC Game

Half-Life

StarCraft

Gaming in the 1990s on the PC was good. In fact, it was so good that many of the games that came out for home computers in this decade are still topping Best Game of All Time lists today! In just about every genre, the 1990s was an era of masterpieces, classic characters, and moments, and you won't go wrong picking up any game on this list to play today. In fact, many have been remade and updated for modern gamers!

YEAR	GAME	GENRE	WHAT MAKES IT AWESOME
1989-1999	*Sim series*	Builder/strategy/more	Starting with *SimCity* in 1989, the Maxis company has released dozens of *Sim* games, simulating everything from city creation, to farming, to theme parks, to an entire planet's life and more.
1990-1997	*Monkey Island series*	Action-adventure	The adventures of pirate Guybrush Threepwood were considered a must-play by PC gamers with a sense of humor and a head for puzzles.
1990-1998	*Quest for Glory series (II-V)*	Adventure/RPG	Praised for their rich settings and combination of point-and-click, story-driven role-playing, and statistics-based action with extensive combat.
1990-1998	*King's Quest series (V-VII)*	Adventure/point-and-click	In the same vein as the *Quest for Glory* series, but with a focus fully on puzzle solving and story instead of having combat mixed in. Where the characters in *Quest for Glory* were nameless and had statistics and a class chosen by the player, *King's Quest* games had the player controlling a character with a name and a story, as well as a personality.

YEAR	GAME	GENRE	WHAT MAKES IT AWESOME
1991-1993	*Duke Nukem series*	Side scrolling shooter/ platformer	Edgy and later controversial, this was one of the standout action games in the early '90s for the PC.
1991-1999	*Civilization series*	Strategy game/ civilization builder	A strategy game that focused on an entire civilization as it went from its birth to the modern day and beyond. Has been one of the preeminent PC series since.
1992	*Dune II*	Real-time strategy	The game that made the genre popular.
1992	*Wolfenstein 3D*	First-person shooter	Very early high-excitement FPS, highly influential.
1993	*Doom*	First-person shooter	One of the earliest story- and setting-driven shooters, which inspired most of the rest of the FPS games on this list.
1993	*Day of the Tentacle*	Adventure/ point-and-click	Possibly the highlight of the point-and-click genre, was considered hilarious and beautifully crafted.
1994	*Warcraft*	Real-time strategy	A fantasy RTS that had humble beginnings but from which some of the most popular games of three decades came, in various genres. One of the most popular non-Mario universes in gaming.
1995-1999	*Command & Conquer series*	Real-time strategy	By far the most well-known RTS series in the 1990s, had many different sub-series.
1996	*The Elder Scrolls: Daggerfall*	First-person RPG	The definitive early game in the series that later brought *Morrowind*, *Oblivion*, and *Skyrim*, three of the most popular RPGs of all time. Had a game world of 161,000 square kilometers, which is often still quoted as being the biggest in any game ever.
1996	*Diablo*	RPG	Inspired most other top-down RPG games with a serious and Western fantasy style.
1996-1999	*Quake trilogy*	First-person shooter/ multiplayer	*Quake* started the multiplayer craze on PC and is still spoken of in reverent terms by those who played it in its heyday.
1997	*Ultima Online*	MMORPG	The first very successful massively multiplayer online role-playing game, following a series of successful offline RPGs.
1997	*Age of Empires*	Real-time strategy	Often considered to be the best RTS game of the era, along with *StarCraft*.
1998	*StarCraft*	Real-time strategy	An RTS so beloved that there are still tournaments held to play it today despite a sequel and many other modern RTS games.
1998	*Half-Life (Counter-Strike and Team Fortress Classic)*	First-person shooter/online	The PC game of the '90s. Brought complex story, setting, and physics to FPS games, plus set the bar for online FPS gaming.
1998	*Fallout 2*	RPG	One of the three big classic top-down RPG games along with *Diablo* and *Baldur's Gate II*. Known for influencing postapocalyptic sci-fi more than any other game.
1998-1999	*Unreal, Unreal Tournament*	First-person shooter/horror, online	The *Unreal* series was another that set the bar for FPS gaming, especially with *Unreal Tournament*'s online gameplay.
1999	*Everquest*	MMORPG	The MMO that started the craze of hundreds of thousands of players spending infinite hours playing; nicknamed *Evercrack* because of this.

Best of the Arcade in the 1990s

Street Fighter II

With home consoles and computers taking over from arcades in a major way, you might think that all of the best games of the 1990s were found in people's homes, but you'd be wrong! Though not at the height it once was, the arcade was still going strong in the 1990s, and these are some of the games that people still flooded with quarters in that decade.

Time Crisis

YEAR	GAME	IMPORTANT MILESTONES AND NEAT FACTS
1991	*Street Fighter II*	The definitive fighting game that most other 2D fighting games are inspired by.
1992	*Mortal Kombat*	The game that brought about the ratings system for video games because of its violence. It spawned a long-lasting series of games as well as many movies, TV shows, and other forms of entertainment.
1993	*Virtua Fighter*	Early version of a fighting game with 3D polygon graphics.
1994	*Sega Rally Championship*	Featured different friction and handling for different driving surfaces, something new in the genre.
1994	*Virtua Cop*	One of the first shooter games to use 3D polygon graphics.
1996	*The House of the Dead*	Took the 3D light gun game and made it very popular with a horror setting.
1996	*Time Crisis*	Another light gun game, this one added a way to duck behind cover, making shooter games more tactical.

The House of the Dead

Sixth Generation Hardware: A New Player Enters, An Old Player Leaves

There was no question that the PlayStation was the biggest, baddest force in video games in the 1990s, but with tech improving and computer games starting once more to pull away from console games in quality, especially when it came to online gaming, it was time for another generation of consoles to step up and claim their space.

SEGA DREAMCAST — 1998

Things kicked off before the millennium even passed with an entry from Sega in 1998, the Dreamcast, which was the very first console to come with a built-in modem to connect to the Internet. This and its fancy 128-bit hardware (once again doubling the last generation's) made this new machine popular for a short time, but Sega found that its audience had grown much smaller after their 32X and Saturn consoles of the last generation had disappointed people.

SONY PLAYSTATION 2 — 2000

The year 2000 brought the PS2, which was an improvement on the PlayStation in every way: It was far more powerful (128 bits, like the Dreamcast), took DVDs—a format that held several times the storage capacity of the last generation's CDs—and it even played DVD movies and music CDs, meaning it could be an all-in-one home entertainment system. And if that wasn't enough, the thing's all-black design just looked cool. Its exclusive games, like *Final Fantasy X* and *Shadow of the Colossus*, were the must-have games of the day, meaning the PS2 was a massive hit.

FUN FACT!

Or maybe not so fun! In the year 2000, the entire country of China banned video game consoles and games out of fear that they were corrupting its population. Despite this, many people were still able to sneak them in, and in a bit of true irony, most consoles were manufactured in China.

NINTENDO GAMECUBE — 2001

Nintendo, as it had in the battle between the N64 and the PlayStation, tried to enter the market to compete—but it did so a year after the PS2 was already out, and suffered for it. Their new console, the GameCube, also didn't feel or look as high-tech or mature as the PS2 in many ways: It was smaller, used much smaller discs, had graphics that weren't much better than the N64, and it came in a purple color with small controllers. Though it still had the hardcore Nintendo fans captured and a whole host of first-party games with Mario and Nintendo's other beloved characters, it simply could not compete with the massive, beautiful, mature games on the PS2.

MICROSOFT XBOX — 2001

Microsoft knew that the PS2 was going to be hard to beat, but in 2001 they put out a machine that used their own operating system's powerful DirectX gaming software and sold their console at a loss in order to secure a foothold in the market. They called it the Xbox (named after DirectX). Because it was based on the code that went into their computers, it was easy to create ports for computer games on the Xbox, and with Microsoft's enormous wealth and experience backing it, the opportunity for the Xbox to shove its way into the market was good. And with the release of a game called *Halo: Combat Evolved*, the first masterpiece FPS on consoles, the Xbox did just that. *Halo* was the game of the generation—an entirely new universe and characters, a genre that had not yet been perfected on the console, and nail-biting head-to-head multiplayer gameplay that fans were ravenous for.

PlayStation Wins

Despite *Halo* and some other great titles, and though it allowed them to establish themselves in the marketplace, Microsoft and the Xbox did not even sell a fifth of the units that the PlayStation 2 did. In fact, the Xbox's 24 million units sold over its lifetime combined with the GameCube's 22 million units were not a third of what PlayStation 2 sold. With 150 million units sold until 2011, the PlayStation 2 was undeniably the bestselling console of all time.

MMORPGs and Competitive Shooters

Call of Duty: Modern Warfare

People have played games over a wired connection to another computer since the 1960s, and each decade since then has had its share of networked gaming. But the Internet suddenly became accessible to the masses in the 2000s, when dial-up modems were a thing of the past. This connectivity catapulted online gameplay, and led to the invention of the Massive Multiplayer Online Role-playing Game (MMORPG). In this new world of connected gaming, two big genres drove people online to play against, and with, each other in the millions online.

The FPS (First-Person Shooter)

Since the days of *Quake,* FPS games were practically synonymous with online gameplay. Shooting a bunch of computer-controlled aliens was fun, yeah, and sometimes that's all you wanted to do. But shooting a bunch of characters controlled by other players was thrilling, because you knew there were other players somewhere in the world on the other side of those characters. Throughout the 2000s, this trend would explode. The PC had games like *Unreal Tournament*, new versions of *Counter-Strike* and *Team Fortress*, and co-op games like *Borderlands*. Consoles had the *Halo* series, which may well be credited for raising the popularity of the console FPS to rival that of the PC, and the *Call of Duty* series, which transitioned from a single-player-focused game to one that was primarily meant to be played online.

The RPG (Role-Playing Game)

The other great movement to online gameplay came in the form of the role-playing game. Since the earliest text-based RPG, people had found ways to get other human players into their game worlds, but widespread access to the Internet made this genre explode. One of the best and most popular examples of this was released by a company called Blizzard in 2004. The game was called *World of Warcraft*.

World of Warcraft

World of Warcraft

In *WoW*, players would create a character by choosing one of two warring factions, a race of mythological creatures within that faction, and a class within that race. *World of Warcraft* was like a mighty beast being set loose on the planet's gaming community—millions were willing to pay not only for the game itself, but for the subscriber fee it takes to keep an account in the game world. People and critics loved everything about it—the graphics, the setting, the quests, the combat, the competition—layering award after award on the game, and by 2010, the game peaked at an incredible twelve million active player accounts. In all, Blizzard says that one hundred million accounts have been made. Even today, over ten years after its release, the numbers sit above seven million active players, with new content continuing to be released.

WoW truly changed the market and the way that the world looked at online gaming. There was both over-obsession (with some stories of players refusing to leave their computer for weeks at a time) and heavy backlash to this highly addictive, highly fun type of game, but at the end of the day people just plain loved *WoW*, and it spawned an entire generation of other MMORPGs. These included some decent hits like the superhero-themed *City of Heroes*, and the *Guild Wars* games, but despite *WoW* laying the groundwork, no other game ever got even a tiny bit close to rivaling *WoW*'s user base or moneymaking capabilities.

The MMORPG genre would start to lose most of its steam by the end of the decade (except for the eternal *WoW*), but this trend of flocking to the Internet to play games with other people was something that would not go away one bit, and would in fact make a massive impact on other genres in the upcoming years.

Video Games Branch Out

Video games have always crossed over into other segments of popular culture. Clothes and toys featuring favorite video game characters have existed since the early days of Nintendo. And, believe it or not, there was even a Billboard top-ten hit song called "Pac-Man Fever" in 1981. But the 2000s were a whole other story when it came to games influencing other cultural products.

Mortal Kombat movie

Video Games Go Hollywood

Take a look at major motion pictures based on video game universes: Before the 2000s, there were only six such big-time films ever released, and only one grossed over $100 million (1997's *Mortal Kombat: Annihilation*). In the 2000s alone, that number went up to seventeen, with five $100-million-grossing films, three that barely missed that mark, and one that pulled in a whopping $275 million in ticket sales. That film was *Lara Croft: Tomb Raider*, starring then queen of the big screen Angelina Jolie. In addition to the *Tomb Raider* films, the 2000s saw series like *Max Payne*, *Silent Hill*, *Hitman*, *Alone in the Dark*, and, perhaps most successfully, *Resident Evil*, make the power of gaming known at the box office in a big way.

Video Games Go Mobile

The iPhone was released in the year 2007, starting another gaming revolution with its worldwide popularity and incredibly powerful hardware. In Japan, the mobile phone had been much more popular and thus more powerful for the whole of the decade, and even in the early 2000s, complex games were huge hits on these early smartphones. Games in the puzzle and virtual pet genres were especially popular, as were arcade-style games and remakes of old arcade games.

When the smartphone went international with the iPhone, and soon after the Android, it took all of about five minutes for longtime video game players and new gamers alike to make mobile gaming an unquestioned success. In 2008, in fact, half of the sales on Apple's App Store were mobile games.

Angry Birds: The World's First Mobile Hit

The world's first massive mobile hit was soon to follow, with 2009 seeing the release of what would become another iconic video game franchise complete with toy lines, a film, and more: *Angry Birds*. A simple physics game that took lessons from Mario and friends by including adorable, recognizable characters, *Angry Birds* was bought 10 million times by 2010. That was just a drop in the bucket compared to what was to come, however: Changing to a free-to-play format with in-app purchases, *Angry Birds* and its many sequels and spin-offs were downloaded over three billion times by 2015, making it one of the most widely played games of any generation on any platform.

Other games that did well in the era stuck to the simple skill-based puzzle or strategy formulas, such as *Pocket God* and *Guitar Hero III*, but it would be in post-2010 that the mobile platform would skyrocket as one of the most lucrative and popular in the world.

The Seventh Generation: Casual vs. Hardcore

The seventh generation of consoles may be one of the most interesting stories in gaming history. This era defined the modern division between the two types of gamers—casual and hardcore. Previously, hardcore gamers had the greatest influence on the market. In a surprising turn of events, casual gamers grabbed the reins of influence.

Handheld Systems

This gen started off with a new trend, which was two competing systems being released within months of each other. These were the handheld entries in the generation, the Nintendo DS and the Sony PlayStation Portable, each of which continued to follow its parent company's approach to console design. The DS had a ton of fun games with Nintendo characters and a brand-new, unique control system featuring two screens, one of which was touch sensitive. The PSP, on the other hand, was the most powerful handheld device yet, with graphics equivalent to major consoles of the previous generations (and got even better as the device aged) and the ability to play games that previously would have only been available with a full console.

Each machine appealed to a certain core type of gamer who was either into cute and/ or casual games or to the gamer who was into high graphic values and mature themes, and also to an ever-present but growing segment of gamers who crossed over between the two, and both systems were huge successes. The PSP sold 80 million units over its manufacturing run, a big feat, though the DS handily outdid even that big number, with 154 million units sold as of late 2014. Partially, Nintendo's bigger numbers can be attributed to releasing many different models of DS and keeping them under the same DS brand name, while PlayStation replaced the PSP with the Vita, but it also showed something that would be very important to the home console battle of the 2000s as well: Casual games now had at least as much draw in the market as hardcore games did, and they often had more.

This divide would be shown to the world in a big way soon, but first the console wars would have a different focus when they got into full swing in late 2005-2006 with the release of the Xbox 360 and then the PlayStation 3.

Both of these machines were essentially just more powerful, fancier versions of the previous generation of consoles, but as always, tech had expanded so fast that the difference between sixth- and seventh-generation games was tremendous. First off, true high-definition graphics were finally available, with HDMI ports on both machines, and each also worked incredibly well with home networks, both in terms of hardware and in terms of software to use online. Games could connect to the Internet as easy as pie, and with a big hard drive on both machines, players could also purchase and download games straight from the 'net without having to buy anything physical or go anywhere. Both consoles also ended up putting a heavy focus on running streaming software for services like Hulu, Netflix, and Twitch, meaning the days of the DVD player were truly at an end.

Both of these machines were super high end, meaning they were also very expensive. In fact, the PS3 was the most expensive console at launch since the Panasonic 3DO, retailing for about $700. The Xbox's cheaper (though still costly) price and excellent set of early games like *Call of Duty 2*, *Gears of War*, and *The Elder Scrolls: Oblivion* (the most advanced FPS, third-person shooter, and RPG games to date) meant that it won the early battle for dominance in the market, the first time that Sony was not in the lead since the PlayStation of the '90s. Later, however, the PS3 would jump back ahead of Microsoft with a new slim model and fancy Move motion controls.

But neither of these hardcore, mature-focused gaming machines could compete with the other entry into the market. Releasing late again (though just a bit behind the PS3), Nintendo dropped the Wii console on the world in late 2006, revealing an entirely new type of controls that was both very modern and entirely unintimidating. These were the Wii's motion controllers, basically rectangles with buttons that were meant to be held in either one hand or both and which responded to the player moving them around. Nothing like this had ever been seen on a home console, and the fact that it was around $200 instead of the much higher prices of the other two consoles meant that, despite barely having more power than the GameCube and having almost exclusively casual games at launch, the Wii sold like hotcakes.

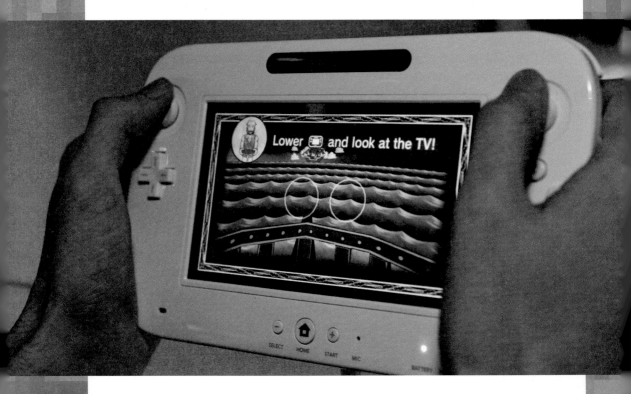

It was surprising to just about everyone, but it made sense as soon as you played one: The Wii was just plain fun. Overturning all trends of the previous ten years and what all of the longtime gaming community believed would happen, the Wii outsold both the Xbox 360 and the PlayStation 3 heavily, moving 100.3 million units worldwide to the 360's 84 million and the PS3's 80 million.

What's interesting to note, however, is that if you compare this era to the early days of consoles, or even the early '90s, none of the major consoles had a true failure in the 2000s. Though some sold better, and Nintendo thoroughly "won" the decade by sales numbers both in handheld and home consoles, all consoles sold well and made hundreds of millions of dollars. In fact, the trend was now set that most gaming households had at least two of the major consoles—if not all three—and often had a handheld and games on the computer to boot.

FUN FACT The 2000s saw a trend in budgets for games getting even bigger. So-called "triple-A" games, or very expensive games that have a ton of work put into them by a large team, now regularly cost hundreds of millions of dollars to develop. Including marketing, the most expensive of the decade was 2009's *Call of Duty: Modern Warfare 2*, which, adjusting for inflation, cost a total of $275 million, but which made over $1 billion by 2010.

Tech Trends in the New Millennium

That technology—it just keeps getting weirder and cooler! The 2000s brought literally game-changing trends that helped to define gaming's biggest decade yet:

WEIRD CONTROLLERS AND GAMES THAT USE THEM

Including the motion controllers of the Wii, there were dozens of odd new peripherals that came out for consoles in the 2000s, often used for just one or two games. This included the guitars of the *Rock Band* and *Guitar Hero* games, the "DK Bongos" of *Donkey Konga*, the dance pads for the console versions of *Dance Dance Revolution*, and the PlayStation's Move motion controllers. The Kinect exemplified this in an entirely different way, being Microsoft's attempt to bring camera-controlled action to the Xbox.

MODE 2 MODE 3 MODE 4

CLOUD COMPUTING BECOMES A THING

Initially, cloud computing simply meant being able to save information to or download information from a game company's servers, but by the end of the 2000s it was becoming a whole different thing. Using the lightning-fast Internet of the day, people were actually able to stream games live to a PC and have little to no delay. The game itself would run on a powerful server computer and not on yours at home, meaning you could run games that were much more complex or had higher settings. Almost like magic!

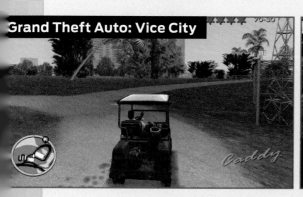

Grand Theft Auto: Vice City

Crash Bandicoot

GRAPHICS: NOT JUST POLYGONS ANYMORE!

Super-powerful graphics processors took the chunky polygonal 3D of the '90s and smoothed it out nice and fine in the 2000s, so much so that by the end of the decade, people were actually able to create game cutscenes where some things were hard to distinguish from real life. You could still do it, but if you were sleepy you could be tricked!

PC Gaming: Taking a Backseat, but Still Hardcore

Company of Heroes

Machinarium

With all of the advances in consoles of the 2000s, the shooter, action-adventure, and RPGs were no longer better on the PC. In fact, many die-hard PC-only gamers found themselves converting to consoles just because the games would be guaranteed to run decently and look great. Many FPS games, for instance, had much larger player bases on console than on PC.

Many types of games still needed to be played with a mouse and keyboard, though, and these were where the PC thrived. MMORPGs, RTS games, top-down strategy games, and, perhaps biggest of all, *The Sims* series, were all going strong in the 2000s. Countless titles like *Baldur's Gate II* (often still called the best game of all time, period, on many critics' lists), *Crusader Kings II*, *Company of Heroes*, and of course *World of Warcraft* were hailed as masterpieces of their genres.

The Sims was another story entirely. The first volume of this game came out in February 2000 and featured no combat, no traditional puzzles, no adventure, no racing, no flying, no real resources, and no jumping—most other games had at least one of these. Instead, you simply live out the characters' mostly normal lives, doing chores and going to work and making dinner. This sounded crazy to many. But gamers love to imagine themselves being other people, so it's no surprise that it was one of gaming's biggest hits ever. It sold 11.3 million copies for the PC in 2002, becoming the bestselling PC game of all time. It also spawned three main sequels and so many expansion packs that it's hard to count, and overall the series has sold over 175 million copies.

Angry Birds

Obviously the PC was not dead (and it won't ever be), but another, much smaller-scale trend happened in the PC market at this time specifically as a reaction against massive console games: the rapid growth of the indie game industry. In the 2000s, getting into game design was no longer as easy as being smart and having the skills; you had to work your way up in giant corporations, and it was rare for someone to actually get to work on the games they had in their head, or to do them the way they wanted to. There were too many other factors in the way, and too much money at stake for that. But game developing tools for the PC were becoming better and cheaper, so a small set of determined developers started creating and releasing games all on their own, often out of their own homes or garages. These games came in all shapes and sizes, in all genres, and sometimes outside any established genre, and they were often sold very cheaply as digital downloads online. Though at the time these games couldn't make the same kind of money that triple-A titles could, their small teams and small budgets meant that more of the money they did make went straight into the developers' pockets. That meant more games could be made, and the cycle continued until indie games became a true force in the industry. Games like *Braid*, the beautiful adventure game *Machinarium*, and *Plants vs. Zombies* were all indie games that made it huge. Even *Angry Birds* was a small indie game when it first came out!

Major Games of the 2000s

The 2000s were a period unlike any other up until that point in gaming. Now that games had very much recovered from the crash of the '80s and were fully cemented as a massive industry, they started coming out in droves. Computers and consoles became tremendously powerful, and the games did, too. Of all the games listed in this book, the games from this period are ones that you most likely have not played many of, but which are absolutely still worth playing because they tend to have graphics and gameplay that still hold up very well to the modern player.

YEAR	GAME	GENRE
2000	Deus Ex	Action RPG/FPS
2000	Diablo II	Action RPG/hack-and-slash
2000	Baldur's Gate II: Shadows of Amn	Isometric RPG
2000-2006	Hitman series	Stealth
2000-2007	Paper Mario series	RPG
2000-2009	The Sims series	Life simulation
2000-2009	Total War series	RTS
2001	Empire Earth	RTS
2001	Red Faction	First-person shooter
2001	Luigi's Mansion	Action-adventure
2001, 2003	Max Payne series	Third person action-adventure/shooter
2001, 2004	RuneScape	MMORPG
2001, 2004	Pikmin series	RTS
2001-2005	Civilization series	Civilization simulation
2001-2006	Black & White series	God game
2001-2007	Tom Clancy's Ghost Recon series	Military tactical shooter
2001-2009	Grand Theft Auto series	Action-adventure/driving/RPG/shooter
2001-2009	Animal Crossing series	Community simulation
2001-2009	Tropico series	City builder/resource management
2001-current	Halo series	First-person shooter
2002	Warcraft III: Reign of Chaos	RTS
2002-2006	Dungeon Siege series	RPG
2002-2006	Tom Clancy's Splinter Cell series	Stealth/third-person action shooter
2002-2008	SOCOM series	Third-person tactical shooter
2002-2009	Ratchet & Clank series	Action-platformer
2003	Defense of the Ancients	Multiplayer online battle arena
2003	Rise of Nations	RTS
2003, 2005	Star Wars: Knights of the Old Republic series	Turn-based RPG
2003-2009	Call of Duty series	First-person shooter
2004	Star Wars Battlefront	First-person shooter/dogfight flying

Game: Halo series

Year: 2001-current · Creators: Bungie originally, other developers later
Genre: First-person shooter

Why it's important: The original *Halo* is known not only as the game that made the Xbox a hit, it's also the game that truly brought excellence in first-person shooter games to the console in general. With the updated tech of the Xbox and a design that meshed perfectly with the thumbstick controller, *Halo* made co-op and local multiplayer first-person shooter games much more accessible. Before this, each player typically had to own his or her own PC and connect to another on a network. *Halo* had it all: a stylish and unique universe, gameplay that was simple to pick up but hard to master, both excellence in single and multiplayer, an array of vehicles and weapons to rival any other game, and an iconic character in the Master Chief that would go on to become one of video gaming's most recognizable. Since the original *Halo: Combat Evolved* game, *Halo* has continued to be the flagship title for the Xbox series of consoles and is considered a classic series.

HOT FACT!

Halo has been so popular with each of its major releases that the term "*Halo* killer" has developed, meaning a game that's popular and good enough to dethrone *Halo* as the best console shooter.

Major Games of the 2000s

YEAR	GAME	GENRE
2004	*World of Warcraft*	MMORPG
2004	*Red Dead Revolver*	Action RPG
2004	*Half-Life 2*	First-person shooter
2004-2008	*Fable series*	Action RPG
2005	*Psychonauts*	Platformer
2005	*Shadow of the Colossus*	Action-adventure
2005	*F.E.A.R.*	Survival horror/first-person shooter
2005-2008	*God of War series*	Action-adventure/hack-and-slash
2005-2009	*Guitar Hero series*	Rhythm
2005-2009	*Football Manager*	Sports management simulation
2005-2009	*Forza Motorsport series*	Racing simulation
2006	*Company of Heroes*	RTS
2006	*Wii Sports*	Casual sports
2006	*Dead Rising*	Open world survival/zombie action-adventure
2006	*The Elder Scrolls: Oblivion*	First-person RPG
2006,2008	*Gears of War series*	Third-person shooter
2007	*Super Mario Galaxy*	Platformer
2007	*Portal*	First-person puzzle/platformer
2007	*The Witcher*	Action-adventure/RPG
2007	*BioShock*	First-person shooter
2007	*Rock Band*	Rhythm
2007	*Mass Effect*	Action RPG/third-person shooter
2007, 2009	*Uncharted series*	Third-person action-adventure/platformer/shooter
2007, 2009	*Assassin's Creed series*	Stealth/action-adventure
2008	*Fallout 3*	Action RPG/first-person shooter
2008	*Mirror's Edge*	Action-adventure/platformer
2008	*Little Big Planet*	Puzzle/platformer/creation
2008	*Mario Kart Wii*	Casual racing
2008, 2009	*Left 4 Dead*	First-person shooter/co-op zombie survival horror
2009	*Bayonetta*	Action/hack-and-slash
2009	*Dragon Age: Origins*	RPG
2009	*inFamous*	Action-adventure
2009	*Borderlands*	First-person shooter/action RPG
2009	*League of Legends*	MOBA

Game: Half-Life 2

Year: 2004 · Creators: Valve Corporation · Genre: First-person shooter

Why it's important: The original *Half-Life* was a revolution in FPS games— it had loads more atmosphere and a deeper story than other shooter games before it, and yet the combat in it was also above and beyond anything else that had ever been released. It was smart, took a ton of skill, and it allowed for players to complete levels in unique and interesting ways. It was a smash hit, and its sequel, *Half-Life 2*, is considered its more refined, better brother. This game had everything, from one of the most realized game worlds to date, to a new physics engine that beat everything that had come before it in terms of feeling realistic. Combat in *Half-Life 2* was frantic and panic-inducing for how realistic it was, but it was also not a game that you could simply plow through, guns blazing, taking tactics and thought to conquer. Of the games in this book, few have ever received as unanimous and loud praise as *Half-Life 2* did when it came out, and in fact, many games based on the Source engine from *Half-Life 2* still are highly popular today, such as *Counter-Strike: GO* and *Team Fortress 2*.

Game: League of Legends

Year: 2009 · Creators: Riot Games · Genre: Multiplayer Online Battle Arena

Why it's important: While *League of Legends* wasn't the first MOBA game, it has certainly become the most popular. In fact, it's the most popular video game in the world as of this writing, with over 70 million players every month and typically over 7.5 million playing at once during peak hours. Its deeply strategic combat takes the 3rd person action-adventure game and meshes it with a real-time strategy style of layout and tactics and throws it all into a multiplayer team-based arena combat setting, and the huge variety of characters, spells, items, and strategies available plus (perhaps most important) the fact that it's free-to-play have made it a tremendous, overwhelmingly successful hit. If you're interested in playing what is absolutely one of the most-played, biggest hits in gaming history that is still running as strong as it ever was, go online and download *LoL* right now, and be prepared to sink a few hundred hours or more into this titan of modern gaming.

HOT FACT!

League of Legends isn't just popular to play; it's also hugely popular to watch! Along with the games *DOTA 2*, *Hearthstone*, and *Counter-Strike: GO*, *League of Legends* has proven to be one of the games that has finally made eSports spectating a truly global and entrenched phenomenon. In fact, about 30 million people watch the LoL World Championship online every year, a number that rivals that of many major traditional sporting championships.

The Eighth Generation: Power to Spare

The seventh generation consoles were powerhouses, and still are. They put everything that came before them to shame when it comes to graphics, processing speed, and the size and complexity of games that they can handle. But the eighth generation of consoles makes the seventh look like child's play. And that's because the tech just keeps getting better, and each time it gets better, it doesn't just get a bit better, or even twice as good. It gets many, many times better.

How Much Better Is Better?

The eighth generation of consoles began in November 2012 with the release of the Wii U and is still in full swing. It's hard to say who's winning, but it's pretty clear that there are only three consoles in the running: the PS4, the Xbox One, and the Wii U.

PS4

One of the three dominant consoles on the market right now is the Sony PlayStation 4 with its "octa-core" (dual quad-core) processors, 8 GB of RAM, and advanced Nvidia graphics unit, and it is said to be ten times more powerful than the PS3 of just one generation ago.

Xbox One

Similar to previous generations, the PlayStation and Xbox libraries are focused on hardcore gaming, giving gamers as much power as possible and preparing for not just the games of today, but the games of the future. With virtual reality a thing that seems to be just around the corner, these consoles are prepping their games and consoles to work with VR headsets, and Sony has even been designing its own, Project Morpheus. All three consoles are also compatible with 3D TVs.

Wii U

The Nintendo offering, the Wii U, once again focuses on unique controller design and a set of games that uses its own well-honed aesthetic and sets of characters to draw users in. The system uses Wii motion controllers plus a special tablet that adds a second screen with motion and touch control.

So far, Xbox and PlayStation have been battling it out for dominance of the generation, while the Wii U has struggled to find its audience, despite a large number of highly rated games such as new titles in the *Mario Party*, *Mario Kart*, and *Super Smash Bros.* series.

This Game's on Fire!

The Witcher III: Wild Hunt is one of the biggest games of the 8th generation. This game has continued three trends in gaming: One, it came from a smaller studio; two, it follows the epic fantasy RPG mold that has been highly popular; and three, it meshes genres and crosses gaming borders by including action-adventure elements, open-world exploration and interaction, highly cinematic storytelling and visuals, and even a collectible card game.

The Witcher III: Wild Hunt

Games Go Indie, and Indie Goes Big-Time

Peasants: 290
Fighters: 34
Varl: 0

43

7

The Banner Saga

Another trend that has become one of the most important in gaming is the popularity of indie games. Indie games have always played a role, but today more than ever before, the indies are playing in the big leagues.

There are now many thousands of indie games out there, including dozens of bonafide hits, such as *Sunless Sea*, *The Banner Saga*, *Fez*, *Terraria*, *Kerbal Space Program*, *The Long Dark*, *Towerfall*, *Hotline Miami*, and so many more it is impossible to count. The appeal of indie games often comes from their resistance to traditional genre classification: They fit into niche genres that don't get much attention from the big companies, mix genres, invent a genre all their own, or are otherwise simply hard to define.

Indie games' detachment from corporations is important for a few other reasons, too. They are often more affordable. You can get three or more indie games online—sometimes far more—for the price of a single big console game, and you know when you do that you're directly supporting the creators of something you like. Additionally, indie games often use the "early access" model, which means that they're put on sale before they're finished for a cheaper price, allowing players to not only play them early, but also to watch them be developed and to even give feedback on that development. This leads to the further benefit of giving developers money to live on and increasing development before the game is even done, meaning more games for everyone!

Gamers have flocked to this model, so much so that in the seventh and eighth generations, big console manufacturers have created ways for indie games to be ported to or even created directly for their consoles. This has led to some indie games becoming console hits already, such as *Rocket League* on the PS4. *Rocket League* is a very simple game that's essentially soccer with cars that can boost. It has become a surprise hit for PS4, a console that is typically used to play much more complicated and expensive games.

Kerbal Space Program

Indie Hit

Kerbal Space Program is a space flight simulator with a massive, passionate fan base, but it's a game that a big studio probably would never make because it is incredibly complex. In the game, players use individual parts to build a spaceship, try to take off without blowing up, and do ever more complex things like calculating orbits and trajectories between planets. *Kerbal*, lacking the attitude and trappings of big corporate games, is instead very cute, quirky, and even buggy.

Minecraft:
An Indie Blockbuster

Minecraft

There is one indie game above all others that has had a huge impact on the industry, becoming the most popular game in the world in the 2010s: It's called *Minecraft*, and it started very humbly. A Swedish programmer named Notch decided to take some of his favorite indie games (primarily *Infiniminer* and *Dwarf Fortress*) and combine them into a game that used very simple graphics but very complex gameplay. The idea: Create an entire game that randomly generates out of blocks that can be broken and/or crafted into other things. Trees drop wood, wood can be turned into pickaxes, pickaxes can mine stone, stone can be turned into houses and ovens and better tools, and so on. Throw in some creatures that either provide food or kill the player and you've added instant excitement, placing the player's buildings and actions at constant risk.

Starting from a very simple early stage in which only a few of these things were implemented, Notch worked on *Minecraft* for a long time, releasing an incomplete version in 2009. As he continued to work and release versions through his company, Mojang, the game grew and grew in popularity with every new added feature.

By the time the game was released as a full version in 2011, it was already a phenomenon, and when it finally came out for smartphones and seventh-generation consoles, its popularity absolutely skyrocketed. All the conditions were right for this to happen: It was a game that parents liked because it was low on violence and high on creativity, plus it was cheap. Kids loved it because they could basically do anything they wanted with it (like LEGO but infinitely easier and more fun), and hardcore and older gamers loved it because spending enough time with it allowed for high levels of creativity and complexity.

Minecraft had one million downloads within a month of its release in 2011. By 2015, it was the most popular game in the world, the number one bestselling PC game and mobile game of all time, and it is behind only *Tetris* and *Wii Sports* in overall sales in the history of video games. Notch sold Mojang in 2014 to Microsoft for $2.5 billion, one of the most lucrative deals in not just video game or entertainment history, but in business history, for a man who simply built an indie game he thought sounded cool.

Looking at those figures and knowing that *Minecraft* started out without any kind of support from game publishers or the game industry, it's obvious that something big has changed in gaming, and what it seems to mean for all of us players is simply more and better games. Which is never a bad thing.

MOBAs and Competitive Games

DOTA 2

Similar to the story of indie games is that of the change in focus of online gaming, away from MMOs and toward new competitive gaming.

When *Warcraft III* came out in 2002, it featured a set of heroes that could be upgraded by killing certain creatures around the map. This would happen while the regular base-building and RTS elements were occurring, but some players decided they liked this part the best. Players took *Warcraft III*'s level editor and some skills with game creation and made a new way of playing the game, based on a map from *StarCraft* called "Aeon of Strife." In this new way of playing, two teams of player-controlled heroes would attempt to destroy the other team's "ancient," a strong building in their corner of the map. Weaker computer-controlled units would spawn every so often for each team and charge at the other team's base, meaning the players had to decide throughout the game whether to defend their base, attack other heroes, attack the other base, or fight the computer-controlled units.

It was called *Defense of the Ancients*, and what started out as a small minigame for *Warcraft III* fans in 2003 quickly blossomed into the primary way that many fans played the game. Eventually it was refined and refined into a very balanced, very complex game played at tournaments. Then the Valve Corporation picked up the rights to *Defense* and made a stand-alone game called *Defense of the Ancients 2*, which made the game even better.

Defense was the first true MOBA game, or multiplayer online battle arena, a new genre whose elements had been used by fans of RTS games for a while. Many MOBAs have been designed since the release of *Defense*, but it was the creation of *League of Legends* in 2009 and then *Defense of the Ancients 2* in 2013 that have changed competitive gaming in a major way.

These two MOBAs have become, behind *Minecraft*, two of the most played games in the entire world for their addictive competitive play. Annual tournaments to find the best players of these games have become the biggest, most watched, and most lucrative video game tournaments, or e-sports, of all time. The *Defense of the Ancients 2* championship, The International, was even broadcast on ESPN and gave out $10.9 million in prize money in 2014—the biggest ever for a gaming competition.

Counter-Strike

Hearthstone

MOBAs are not the only major competitive games, either: FPS games like *Counter-Strike: Global Offensive* are also heavily competitive, with big tournaments and famous players; in 2014, Blizzard released yet another game based on *Warcraft*, this time a competitive collectible card game called *Hearthstone: Heroes of Warcraft*, which has itself already become one of the most popular games in the world, with 30 million registered users as of 2015.

Things have changed quite a bit from the days of grinding to earn neat items and high levels in MMORPGs. Now online gaming is all about getting skilled, being smarter, and winning. Plus, it can actually pay, and there are even colleges in the United States that now offer scholarships to e-sports players just like they do to traditional athletes.

Mobile Games Come of Age

With smartphones getting better and more widely available, the mobile gaming market has expanded rapidly. New hit titles have been released each year since 2010, pulling in over $20 billion in revenue each year, a number that puts mobile gaming on par with consoles.

Having a game in your pocket on something you already need (a smartphone) is much easier than having to sit down and play a game on a dedicated console that costs hundreds of dollars, and so mobile gaming has activated players who weren't already gaming, as well as those who were. Its popularity reveals that just about everyone's a gamer, if you make it easy!

Not surprisingly, the bestselling paid game on smartphones is the mobile version of *Minecraft*, which, because of its simple graphics, is almost the same as the console version. Other popular mobile games, such as *Candy Crush Saga* (puzzle) and *Clash of Clans* (strategy), are two of the best, both pulling in hundreds of millions of dollars every year. *Angry Birds* has also stayed in the game year after year by releasing a huge number of different titles – everything from *Angry Birds Space* and *Angry Birds Fight* to teaming up with brands such as *Star Wars* and *Transformers*. Because it is fairly easy to develop a game for the big smartphone companies, there are hundreds of thousands of other games available to players, in every genre.

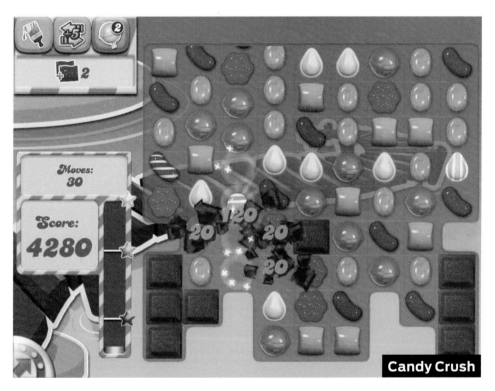

Candy Crush

While the graphics and complexity of mobile games have not even come close to reaching the level of current consoles or PCs, mobile games do represent two things: the largest number of people playing on any gaming platform ever by far, and the largest number of games ever released for any platform.

Classics of Today: Major Games of the 2010s

The Witcher 3: Wild Hunt

BioShock

Who says a game has to be old to be a classic? These days, games sell millions of copies within weeks of release, and we've never seen so many people playing the top games at once as we do right now. On top of that, tech is hitting a point where every new game seems to top the one that came out a week before it. We're still working our way through the 2010s, but here are the top games that have come out so far!

YEAR	GAME	GENRE
2010-current	Telltale Games series	Graphic adventure (not action, not point-and-click)
2010	Civilization V	Civilization simulation
2010	StarCraft II: Wings of Liberty	RTS
2010	World of Tanks	Action MMO
2010	Super Meat Boy	Arcade-style platformer
2010	Mass Effect 2	Third-person action RPG/shooter
2010-2013	BioShock series	First-person shooter
2010-2014	Assassin's Creed series	Action-adventure/semi-stealth
2011	Minecraft	3D action-adventure/survival/builder
2011	Terraria	2D action-adventure/survival/builder
2011	Portal 2	First-person puzzle/platformer
2011	Deus Ex: Human Revolution	First-person action RPG/shooter/stealth
2011	The Elder Scrolls V: Skyrim	First-person action RPG
2011	Batman: Arkham City	Action-adventure
2011, 2014	Dark Souls series	Action RPG

YEAR	GAME	GENRE
2011, 2015	The Witcher series	Third-person action RPG
2012	Candy Crush Saga	Mobile puzzle/arcade
2012	Fez	Platformer/puzzle
2012	Crusader Kings II	Nation simulation ("grand strategy")
2012	Clash of Clans	Resource-based strategy and RTS
2012	FTL: Faster than Light	Top-down strategy/roguelike
2012	Hotline: Miami	Top-down shooter
2012	Diablo III	Action RPG/hack-and-slash
2012	XCOM: Enemy Unknown	Turn-based tactical squad combat
2012	Borderlands 2	FPS/action RPG
2012	Dishonored	Action-adventure/stealth
2012, 2014	Far Cry series	First-person action RPG
2013	The Last of Us	Action-adventure/survival horror
2013	Don't Starve	Survival/builder/action-adventure
2013	Kentucky Route Zero	Adventure/point-and-click
2013	Tomb Raider	Action-adventure/puzzle/stealth
2013	TowerFall	Multiplayer 2D arena game
2013	Dota 2	MOBA
2013	Grand Theft Auto V	Action-adventure/driving/shooter
2013	Papers, Please	Simulation/puzzle
2013	Gone Home	Adventure/interactive fiction
2014	The Banner Saga	Tactical combat RPG
2014	Divinity: Original Sin	Isometric RPG
2014	Super Smash Bros. for Nintendo 3DS/for Wii U	Fighting
2014	Broken Age	Adventure/point-and-click
2014	Nidhogg	Competitive arcade-style fighting game
2014	Alien: Isolation	First-person action-adventure/survival horror
2014	Hearthstone: Heroes of Warcraft	Collectible card strategy game
2014	P.T.	Survival horror
2014	Goat Simulator	Action/humor/sandbox
2014	Jazzpunk	First-person adventure/art game
2015	The Witcher 3: Wild Hunt	Third-person action-RPG
2015	Pillars of Eternity	Isometric RPG
2015	Kerbal Space Program	Space flight simulator/sandbox

The Future of Gaming:
Virtual Reality

Powerful machines, the rise of indies and mobile, new types of competition, and the fact that every new decade in gaming has brought surprises and changes we could never have predicted: The future of gaming is nothing but bright.

There is one change in particular, one incredible piece of technology, that is right around the corner, and it will completely change the way we game in a way that's more drastic than the home console, the beginning of 3D, or any other event in gaming history.

That, gamers, is **virtual reality**: gaming inside of a virtual world. Virtual reality has been a dream for decades, but until now, technology has been too expensive or not powerful enough to create a true virtual experience.

The Microsoft HoloLens

WHAT IS IT? A wireless ("untethered") headset that displays 3D holograms onto your vision of the real world and allows you to interact with these holograms using your hands, vision, and voice.

Technically, the Microsoft entry into this new, exciting world of technology is not actually virtual reality, but what's called "augmented reality." This means that you'll still see the real world when you wear the Microsoft HoloLens, but you'll see 3D images displayed onto it, merging the real world and the virtual into one.

The gaming potential for the HoloLens is enormous: It was announced soon after Microsoft bought the world's biggest game, *Minecraft*, and it is designed to make that game work in all new ways. The HoloLens is smart. It contains an entire Windows 10 computer in the headset. The HoloLens can project images onto surfaces in your environment, so that you can actually project your *Minecraft* game world right onto your living room or dining room table!

PlayStation VR

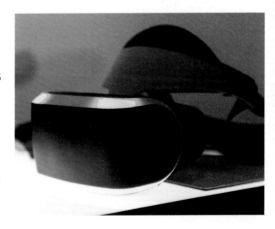

WHAT IS IT? Sony's entry into the VR world that will work automatically with the PS4 and features some of the best sound in VR.

Sony has made a name as the crowned king of technology in the gaming world since the original PlayStation. With the most popular machine in the current generation of video games in the PS4, Sony is not about to sit on the sidelines as VR hits the mainstream.

What makes the PlayStation VR intriguing for gamers is that, unlike the Oculus, it is built specifically to work perfectly with the PS4. So even though the Oculus may be slightly more advanced, it requires a fairly decent PC in good condition. Also, Sony is actively encouraging game designers to create their PS4 games to work with the PlayStation VR unit— to make sure the experience is seamless.

Sony has been in the game for a while when it comes to motion controls and sound equipment, and so your gaming experience overall with the Sony VR will be totally in-depth and amazing.

The Mystery of the Nintendo NX

WHAT IS IT? Nobody is entirely sure yet! But, we do know that Nintendo is hyping a new technology, and many say it will be virtual reality or augmented reality-based.

Nintendo has an interesting position: They aren't known for having the newest or most powerful tech in their products, but they are known for their work with new ways of interacting with games. Many believe that the Nintendo NX will be Nintendo's attempt to make VR "fun," something they have criticized the Oculus and PlayStation VR for not being. If this is the case, expect Nintendo to put out something very inexpensive and thoroughly fun, and to put out a ton of games featuring their best-loved characters like Mario and crew that are built around this device.

Oculus

WHAT IS IT? The Big Daddy of VR, the Oculus was the first real VR headset, and it is the one with the best technology and most excitement built up around it.

The Oculus company was the one that took the idea of VR and brought it to the public with a real, working VR machine. Known as the Oculus Rift, this is the one that people are talking about the most. It has the best screen, it reacts the best to your movements, it has been tested the most, and, maybe most exciting, it's not tied to any particular console developer, so there is a ton of freedom for developers to create games for it.

The Oculus also has the backing of the billions of dollars controlled by Facebook, meaning that there will be all sorts of applications for the device, from gaming and far beyond. While the Oculus machines probably won't be as stable or easy to use as the PlayStation VR, or as cheap as what Nintendo puts out if they enter the market, Oculus VR devices will very likely be the premier VR experience when it comes to mind-blowing uses of this already incredible tech.

Gaming's Bright Future:
Where Will Tech Take Us?

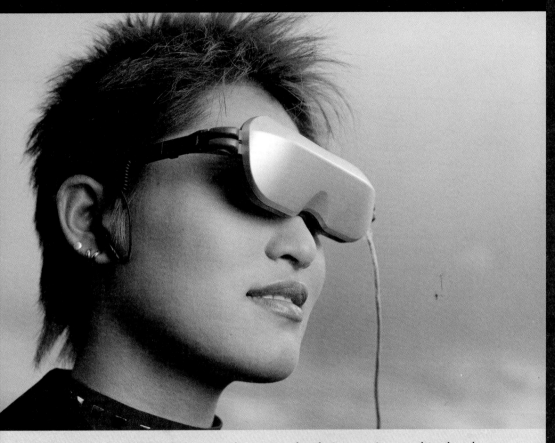

The answer is: Nobody knows, but everybody in gaming and technology can agree on one thing. It's going to be amazing.

The future, to put it bluntly, is going to be incredible. With virtual reality finally arriving, and if games continue to wow us with how big, complex, and realistic they are, and if even small game companies can go on to make $2.5 billion games like *Minecraft*, it seems clear: There is no limit to what games can do, or where they can take us. All we have to do is wait to see what video games will bring us next, and then **push the start button**.

Photo Credits